A Threefold Cord

Couples' Devotionals

by
Bill and Penny Banuchi

Stay wrapped around Him

Bill + Penny Banuchi
3/3/06

Copyright Notice Page

DEDICATION

Penny and I wish to dedicate this work, first of all, to Jesus Christ, the One who gave us the hope, wisdom and power to save our marriage from becoming one of the sad statistics of our time.

Secondly, to all those saints who have helped us through, prayed us through, and loved us through—even when we weren't very lovable—to see this marriage restored, and used for God's glory.

And of course to the hundreds of couples who have allowed us the privilege of being a part of the restoration of their marriages. Their hard work is always an inspiration to us.

Last, but certainly not least, we want to dedicate this work to our children, Dulcinea and Bill Jr., who had to endure the childish antics of parents in marital strife. We thank God for the wonderful man and woman that each has become, more in spite of our parenting than because of it.

TABLE OF CONTENTS

FOREWORD

In a day when families and marriages face challenges as never before, this devotional book provides encouragement for couples to bring every thought, feeling and action into the light of God's truth and love. It is a must for every home!

Bill and Penny have a passion, and a desire to bring unity and wholeness into the lives of couples, marriages and families. They have brought insight to Scripture revealed to them as they strained forward, grappling with circumstances and stresses together as they sought to find balance in their own lives. They present questions that will provoke meaningful times of communication. These insights will help couples and families to stand on the solid rock of the Word of God, our only sure foundation in an unsure world.

Inspiring, and encouraging, these practical devotionals draw us closer to God while strengthening our relationships with one another.

Dr. J. Patrick Fiore
Christian Life Center

PREFACE

These devotionals were first created for our web site to minister to couples beyond our physical reach. It soon became apparent that God was using them to bring healing and restoration to many more couples than we ever could have imagined.

The next step became apparent: put them all together in one book to minister to even more couples. Name it "A Threefold Cord" to illustrate the lives of a couple wrapped around Jesus Christ who must always be at the center of a meaningful, loving relationship. This book is, in effect, an extension of our seminars and counseling ministry.

These devotionals incorporate many of the principles we use in counseling, principles that have resulted in the restoration of marriages that seemed impossible to save, but yet we have seen how our willingness, and God's power can truly work miracles. Individuals are saved. Marriages are reconciled. Families are restored, and God gets the glory!

These devotionals can be an instrument of healing and restoration if you approach them diligently and prayerfully. They may prompt you to seek professional counseling. If so, be sure the counseling you seek is truly Christian. Secular counselors often counsel from a different worldview that places personal happiness as the goal instead of the result of pursuing God.

Find a quiet place and time to share these devotionals together. Commit yourselves to "working" to see your marriage become all God wants it to be for the benefit of the children, your happiness, and ultimately, for God's glory! Use the space at the end of each devotional to journal what God is saying to you about the subject covered.

Please feel free to e-mail your comments or questions to _info@marriageandfamily.org._

A Threefold Cord

Weekly Devotionals for Couples

Week #1

ACCEPTING ONE ANOTHER

"Accept one another, then, just as Christ accepted you, in order to bring praise to God."—Romans 15:7

Can we accept one another just as we are, recognizing that we all fall short of God's glory. Neither one of us can be seen as better or worse than the other. The Scriptures tell us in James 2 that if we transgress the law at just one point we're guilty of transgressing the entire law. It cannot be kept in part. It's all or nothing. Therefore both my spouse and I are equally guilty, but Praise God we are also equally forgiven! That's why it's been said that the ground is level at the cross. Not one of us can stand taller than the other. If we do so, we stand deceived with an attitude of something less than the humility we need to treat each other tender-heartedly and kind.

We need to accept one another, not for what we are, for we all fall short, but for who we are—God's gift to one another. If God were to reach His arm down through the clouds, and say, "Here, I have a gift for you." He opens His hand and there you see a piece of coal. What would you do with that gift? Would you discard it? Treat it irreverently? Would you have contempt for it, because it's only a piece of coal? Or would you value it highly because of who it was that gave you the gift? So it is with your spouse. He or she is not to be valued for what they are, but for who they are—God's gift to you. You may see a piece of coal. God sees a diamond in the making, no different than yourself.

So let's make a decision today to accept one another, just as Christ accepts us, not for what we are, but for who we are: God's gift to one another—*diamonds in the making!*

10

Question to ask each other: Can you truly see me as God's gift to you? Are there certain things you find difficult to accept?

Prayer for both of us: Lord, help us to realize that neither one of us is better than the other. We've all sinned and fall short of Your glory. Help us to accept one another just as we are, as we both struggle to change day by day for the better.

Journal . . .

Week #2

AFFECTION

"I thank my God every time I remember you. In all my prayers for all of you, I always pray with joy because of your partnership in the gospel from the first day until now, being confident of this, that he who began a good work in you will carry it on to completion until the day of Christ Jesus. It is right for me to feel this way about all of you, since I have you in my heart; for whether I am in chains or defending and confirming the gospel, all of you share in God's grace with me. God can testify how I long for all of You with the affection of Christ Jesus. And this is my prayer: that your love may abound more and more in knowledge and depth of insight, so that you may be able to discern what is best and may be pure and blameless until the day of Christ. . . ."

—Philippians 1:3-10

Paul is saying a whole lot here. He seems to be encouraging believers (That's you I hope), to be tenderhearted and kind to one another as we struggle to change day by day. It's like he's saying, "Don't sweat the small stuff. God will take care of it. He will finish the work and set everybody straight. Don't worry about it. Just give yourselves to treating one another with kindness and affection." He's encouraging us to look past the faults. Be ministers of grace. Enjoy the journey. There's no better way to share life's journey than with heartfelt affection, the affection of Christ Jesus.

It begins with the look in your eye. Do your eyes communicate affection to your spouse? Try this: Before you speak to your spouse, think: "I love you." The very spirit of love will come through in the gleam in your eye. Your tone of voice will communicate affection. More important than the words

12

you use, is the spirit behind the words. Let your words be affectionate. How about an affectionate non-sexual physical touch? It must be non-sexual if its to be affection. A touch on the cheek, a stroke on one's shoulder. Whatever form it takes affection says, "I love you. I care for you. I highly desire you. You are special to me." Take the time and make the effort to understand what forms of affection truly minister grace to your spouse. Then give yourself to the challenge.

Let Paul's prayer be answered in your life. Let your love abound more and more with depth of insight that you may be able to look past the faults to see the needs and respond with tenderhearted kindness and affection, because He who began a good work in both of you will carry it on to completion. Praise His Wonderful Name!

Question for both of us: If we were to connect an "affection-ometer" to our relationship how would it look? What forms of affection work for us and what forms don't? Why?

Prayer for both of us: Lord, help us to be tenderhearted and kind to one another; to grow in our ability to demonstrate the affection of Christ to one another that we may enjoy the ride and you may receive all the glory!

Journal . . .

Week #3

"ARE YOU AN OVERCOMER OR A HANGER INNER?"

"For whatever is born of God overcomes the world; and this is the victory that has overcome the world, even our faith."
—1 John 5:4 (NAS)

Do you really feel confident that you will overcome the problems and challenges to your marriage, or do you feel like the problems are forming themselves into a giant snowball at the top of the mountain above you, and as you feel the earth begin trembling beneath your feet you realize you are about to be overcome? Where is this victory that's supposed to overcome the world? As John said, it's our faith. It's our faith in the person of Jesus Christ. It's knowing that He is in control. It's knowing that even if the snowball comes rolling over me, I'll get right back up again and continue my walk with Him. Let the snowball come. I overcome it by His Spirit working in me. Sure, I may get knocked down, but I'll never be knocked out. The only thing these problems may accomplish is to validate my share in the Kingdom. Jesus tells us, "To him who overcomes I will give the right to eat of the tree of life . . ." (Rev. 2:7b). Unfortunately, we can't be overcomers unless we have something to overcome.

Do our marriage problems look like that snowball coming down that mountain? Then it's time to build our faith in Him. Don't even try to stop that coming snowball—or avalanche— without a solid confidence in His faithfulness to help overcome, anger with kindness, selfishness with grace, anxiety with peace, frustration with hope, and everything else with pure, unadulterated love. Resolve in your own heart to never again answer the question, "How are you?" with the answer, "Hanging in there." You were never called to be a "hanger." You were called to be an overcomer. You can only do it with His power working in and through you. So get plugged in to Christ. Let the power of the Holy Spirit surge through you. Then bring on the snowballs; bring on the avalanche. You'll just grow stronger with every one you overcome. Then, give Him the praise!

Question for both of us: Do we feel like overcomers, or do we feel like we're being overcome? Why?

Prayer for both of us: Lord, help us to change our mindset from "hanging in there" to "overcoming". Help us !earn to grow through our problems together, so that what the enemy of our marriage sends to divide us will actually cause us to close ranks against him. We will overcome him together, and grow stronger. Grow our faith in Your boundless goodness and mercy.

Journal . . .

Week #4

A STATE OF BEING

"Be kind and compassionate to one another, forgiving each other, just as in Christ God forgave you."

—Ephesians 4:32

Paul isn't talking about something we should be doing. He's talking about a state of being—a state of continually receiving God's forgiveness in Christ, and passing on that forgiveness to one another. It's a dynamic thing. As you are being forgiven—as the flow of grace passes through you—you can allow it to flow into the lives of one another. This is an active state of being. When you are offended you forgive, because you are in a state of being a channel of forgiveness and grace. Even while you are being offended, you are being forgiving. You're not waiting for your spouse to say, "I'm sorry." You are already giving forgiveness because this is who you are. This is the state of being you are in. You are *being* kind and compassionate and forgiving. Aren't you glad Jesus didn't wait for you to say you were sorry before He hung on the cross? He didn't say, "I'll hang on this cross if you'll repent." He just hung, and offered Himself willingly to "whosoever will." Our love and devotion to Him is a response to that unconditional love and forgiveness He demonstrated. Our spouses' love and devotion to us will also be a response to the unconditional love we have for them.

Are we *being* kind and compassionate, forgiving, even as we are being forgiven? Or are we demanding that our spouse shows remorse before we offer forgiveness? If that's the case, your love is conditional, and you are stopping the flow of grace. Let it flow. Be kind, and compassionate, continually forgiving, no matter what!!

16

Question to ask each other: When do I feel you aren't forgiving?

Prayer for both of us: Lord, help us to receive Your flow of grace and forgiveness for one another, that it might freely flow through us into the lives of each other, unhindered by our selfish demands to see signs of repentance. Help us to be in a state of being kind, compassionate and forgiving, unconditionally, even as You are with us.

Journal . . .

Week #5

A CANCER CALLED ANGER

"Better a patient man than a warrior, a man who controls his temper than one who takes a city."—Proverbs 16:32

Nothing is more devastating to a relationship than residual anger which pops up its ugly head continually at the slightest provocation. An angry person is incapable of having a healthy loving relationship with anyone. Please understand. We all get angry from time to time. That's not the problem. Even Jesus got angry, but in His expression of that anger He didn't sin. The anger isn't the problem. It's how we express that anger that can get us into trouble. If we don't express it properly it can be destructive. If we keep stuffing it inside, eventually it will find its way into every cell of our being until we become an angry person. In other words, it's one thing to be a person who gets angry from time to time. It's another thing to be an angry person. An angry person cannot love. The unresolved anger is a barrier to intimacy. Anger is no longer what you may be feeling. It becomes part of who you are. Unresolved anger is a marriage and family killer.

We need to be honest with ourselves about our anger. Take inventory of yourself to determine if you have residual anger toward anyone, or anything, or even God! Then work toward repentance and forgiveness until that cancer of anger is fully removed and replaced with tenderness and mercy. Then you will be able to feel God's love fully, and receive it for yourself so that you may have it to extend to others around you. Until then, the cancer will continue on its course of destruction.

Question for both of us: How do we handle our anger? Do we blow up in angry outbursts all the time? Do we stuff it in an unhealthy way? Do I have residual anger toward anyone or any past sense of injustice in my life?

Prayer for both of us: Lord, help us manage our anger in a way that is pleasing to You. Help us offer our anger up to You and replace it with Your tenderness and mercy. Help us to persevere until our body, soul and spirit are clean of any residual anger.

Journal . . .

ASSERTIVENESS TRAINING 101

"Surely, you desire truth in the innermost parts."
—Psalm 51:6

This is one of the most crucial factors affecting relationships. Too often, our desire to keep the peace causes us to sacrifice truth. We're afraid of "rocking the boat" so we remain silent rather than expressing how we truly feel. Whenever we sacrifice truth in this way we can be certain there will be a problem, if not today, then in the future. But be assured, it will raise its ugly head, and show up in the form of resentment, bitterness or strife. When we don't express how we truly feel about an issue we send a message by our silence that is not reflective of who we really are, and how we really feel. Therefore, our spouse gets a false impression. You may have peace for now, but it's a peace based on a less than truthful representation of who you are and how you feel. Your partner cannot come to know you until you decide to speak the truth in love. This quality of assertiveness is absolutely vital for a growing, healthy relationship. This is what God desires from us, "truth in the innermost parts . . ." and this is what we need to give one another, even when it means some discomfort. We do need to use wisdom and sensitivity concerning timing, but we do need to share truthfully. When we can speak the truth without anger or being mean-spirited we have the basis for healthy, effective communication.

Question for dialogue: What are some of the issues we have not spoken the truth about in order to keep the peace?

Prayer for both of us: Lord, help us to be courageous enough to speak the truth in love, yet with the wisdom and timing of the Holy Spirit to help us truly know one another.

Journal . . .

BARRIERS TO FORGIVENESS

"For if you forgive men when they sin against you, your heavenly Father will also forgive you. But if you do not forgive men their sins, your father will not forgive your sins."
—Matthew 6:14, 15

When our spouse hurts us, especially over a period of time, we tend to see them no longer as our spouse but as "the one who is hurting me." We subconsciously see ourselves in an adversarial relationship as though our spouse were the enemy against whom we must protect. The first step in being able to forgive (so that we may be forgiven) is to see your spouse not as the one who is hurting you out of a desire to do you ill, but as one who has hurt you because he or she is a flawed weak human being just like you. Hurting people hurt other people. Your spouse hurts you, because their history, or their lack of relationship with Christ, hasn't taught them how to express love. This is particularly true if your spouse doesn't know God. The Bible tells us that he who knows not God simply does not know love for God is love. Let's begin to see one another as God sees us—flawed weak human beings who hurt one another out of their own hurts. Let's begin to forgive, because, we too, need forgiveness to keep the flow of God's grace unrestricted and freely flowing in and through our lives.

Question for both of us: How do I see you, as "the one who is hurting me" or as one flawed weak human being, like myself, struggling to learn how to love?

Prayer for both of us: Lord, help us to see one another as You see us, not as our enemy, or as the one who is trying to hurt me, but as sinners in need of a Savior, struggling together to learn how to love. Help us to know You more so that we may know love.

Journal . . .

Week #8

BE AN ENCOURAGER

"Therefore encourage one another and build each other up, as you are doing."—I Thessalonians 5:11

There may be days when we just want the world to go away. We would rather stay in bed and pull the covers up over our heads than have to deal with life. Thank God Jesus didn't take that attitude. He knew full well in those last days that He would be betrayed, denied three times by one of His closest friends and then crucified (talk about a reason to get the blues!). Yet He would still press on because of His commitment to the Father. Jesus was our Example. He could have called legions of angels to set Him free, but He chose to sacrifice Himself for us, because He loves us. God knows the trials and tribulations of your heart. He knows sometimes you are hurting beyond what you feel you can handle. Sometimes we must do as King David did when there was no encouragement to be found anywhere. He encouraged himself in the Lord. Our Heavenly Father is right there to hold our hand, to hug us, and to lift our chin so we can concentrate on Him. As we press forward into our day, let us think of our spouse, our children. How can we, as servants of the Lord, children of the Most High, imitate Christ, and encourage ourselves in the Lord, then bring words of encouragement to them? Study your spouse, and your children. Then ask God to let the gift of encouragement be stirred up within so that you may be a blessing to someone else, instead of a lump under the sheets doing good for no one. Encourage yourself in the Lord, and then encourage another.

Question for both of us: When are there times that you need particular encouragement? How can I encourage you better?

24

Prayer for both of us: Lord, help us to be encouragers, uplifters, not discouragers and wet blankets. Help us to be a blessing to one another, and a reminder of the wonderful life we have in You.

Journal . . .

BIGGER THAN BOTH OF US

"Remember the Lord, who is great and awesome, and fight for your brothers, your sons and your daughters, your wives and your homes"—Nehemiah 4:14b

Nehemiah was speaking these words to his generation as they were preparing to rebuild the walls of Jerusalem in the midst of opposition in order to let them know that this was not just about their self-interests. This was about fighting for something greater than themselves. It was about their marriages, their families and their nation.

As we look around to see the breakdown of the American family it becomes clear that it is, once again, time to fight for our marriages our families and our nation. This is no time to let our pettiness keep us from closing ranks against the outside enemies of marriage and family. It's time to quit whining and fighting about meaningless issues. It's time to love one another as Christ loved us—just as we are—and let that love flow into a world searching for answers in all the wrong places. It's time to let our children see the love of God in us. It's time to impact our communities for righteousness' sake. If we don't, our children will rise up to curse us for handing them a world in much worse shape than the world our parents handed us. Will our children rise up to bless us, or curse us? The answer will be determined by the choices we make today.

Question for both of us: In what ways have we let our self-interests keep us from allowing God's love to freely flow into the lives of others? What other couple can we help today,

26

even by doing something as simple as sharing these devotionals with them?

Prayer for both of us: Lord, help us to set aside our selfishness and pride, to love each other, unconditionally, as You love us. Help us to reach out to another couple or family in trouble. Help us to be a light in a dark world. Empower us to fight for our marriage, our family and our nation.

Journal . . .

Week #10

COMMUNICATE YOU CARE

"I am the good shepherd. The good shepherd lays down his life for the sheep. The hired hand is not the shepherd who owns the sheep. So when he sees the wolf coming, he abandons the sheep and runs away. Then the wolf attacks the flock and scatters it. The man runs away because he is a hired hand and cares nothing for the sheep. I am the good shepherd; I know my sheep and my sheep know me."—John 10:11-14

This week we had another couple that had a major breakthrough in their relationship. Suddenly, strife is gone! They are actually talking to each other, and moreover, they're enjoying it. They are actually enjoying being with each other. That's something that hasn't been true for years! When I asked the wife what made the difference she said, "He is so different. He's not angry all the time. He's talking to me nicely, and doing things that show he's really trying." Then I asked the husband what he thought the difference was. He said, "I realize I have to do only one thing. Communicate that I care." That's the key. Not only to care, but to communicate effectively that you care. That's why when Jesus spoke about the Good Shepherd He said not only will the Good Shepherd lay down His very life for His sheep, but His sheep will know Him. They will know He cares. That's why they listen to His voice. He communicates that He cares. Are we being as The Good Shepherd or are we being as the hired hand, running off into our own little world of isolation while our marriages and families are lost to the wolves of this culture?

It's simple, but not natural. It takes a conscious decision to choose to communicate you care. It's not enough to care if you can't effectively communicate it. It could be argued that if you don't care enough to communicate you care, you really just don't care. Ponder that one.

You, too, can have that breakthrough in your relationship. Put everything else on the back burner until you can effectively communicate you care. Be as the Good Shepherd, not the hired hand.

Question for both of us: How well do we communicate we care? What do our attitudes and tone of voice say about how much we care?

Prayer for both of us: Lord, help us to communicate we care. Help us to overcome our natural tendencies to react defensively, or with a negative attitude. Help us to let our spouse know, even when we don't understand or agree, that we care. Help us be as The Good Shepherd.

Journal . . .

Week #11

EMPTY NEST

"And this is my covenant with them says the Lord, 'My spirit will not leave them, and neither will these words I have given you. They will be on your lips and on the lips of your children and your children's children forever, I, the Lord, have spoken!'"—Isaiah 59:21

It is a difficult time when a child leaves home. Some of us are already experiencing "The Empty Nest Syndrome." The real tragedy is that if we haven't been working on our marriage all along that nest will be filled with total emptiness when the children are gone.

We all hurt in our own ways when a child goes off to college, or simply decides it's time to go on his or her own. We're facing this now. Our son has moved out, because he simply decided it was time for him to be on his own, and our daughter will be getting married in a couple of months, and she too, will leave the nest. My first thought, particularly as a mom, is "My babies, how will we make it without them?" Then we begin thinking of the trials they will face without us to help them out. The reality is *I miss my child!* The hurt is felt in various ways, and the tears are shed at various times. That's normal. But if we do not remember who they really belong to recovery will take significantly longer.

Children are a blessing from God. They belong, not to us, but to Him. He blesses us by lending them to us for a season. We do the best we can loving, teaching, nurturing, training and enjoying them. Then, before we know it time is up. It's difficult to face the thought of releasing them into the world as it

30

is today. Only our faith in God, and His promise to watch over them makes it manageable. If we've taken the time to train them up in the way they should go, they won't depart from it. Now, just what that particular journey looks like is different for each individual. Only God knows the way each one should go. The one thing we can count on is God's promise to spread His wings over our children to keep them in the safety of His presence.

Questions for both of us: How are we training our children? Are we the example that shows the children that God, and submission to His Word must be first? Do they see Christ in us? Why, why not?

Prayer for both of us: Dear God, please help us to have the wisdom to train our children in Your ways. Please help us to ask forgiveness whenever we are wrong, and give us a right spirit to pass on to them. Help us to glorify You in the way we take care of the gift You have entrusted to us for a season— our children. Then help us to trust You for their safety when they leave the nest. Draw them ever closer to Yourself.

Journal . . .

Week #12

EXPECTATIONS

"The wages of sin are death, but the gift of God is eternal life in Christ Jesus, our Lord."—Romans 6:23

C. S. Lewis said that "there is nothing better than a Christian who knows himself, and no Christian who knows himself would dare think that he deserves anything better than hell."

Talk about getting knocked off of your self-righteous high horse! But C. S. Lewis was just communicating the Gospel truth that if we received what we truly deserve we would all be burning in hell. Everything else is a bonus. Now, if we can translate that into everyday expectations we can begin to appreciate one another for what we are—a gift of God's grace—a bonus! The reason we tend to take one another for granted is because we expect more than what we deserve. It's that simple. If we can adjust our expectations we can increase our sense of appreciation for one another and be a lot happier. Here's what happens. If I expect dinner to be on the table at 6 o'clock sharp each night, when it's there I don't make a big thing of it because, after all, it's expected. If it isn't there, look out! I get angry because I didn't get what I thought I deserved, and everybody pays! Now if I don't expect dinner to be on the table, and it's not there, I'm not upset, because I didn't expect it anyway. If it is on the table, wow, what a bonus! I can appreciate it because I didn't expect it. Apply the same principle to sex, and every other part of your relationship, and you'll see that most of your anger and frustration comes because you're not getting something you expect, which you think you have a right to. Lower your expectations of one another. If you expect nothing, then everything will be received as a gift. Your heart will reflect gratitude and appreciation, and create an atmosphere of grace. When you expect everything you don't see the positives but only the negatives. When you don't expect anything, you don't see the negatives but only the positives. That's where we want to be. Be careful not to insist on what you deserve. You might get it as C. S. Lewis reminds us. Whatever you have now, it's a lot more than what you deserve. Be grateful. Be thankful, and begin working together from that place of mutual appreciation. Make no expectations or demands, but receive one another as a gift of God's grace.

Question for both of us: What kind of expectations do we have of one another that continually cause us to feel disappointment and frustration? What can we realistically expect?

Prayer for both of us: Lord help us to realize that the only thing we deserve is hell, and that everything else is a gift of Your grace, especially our mates. Help us to place no expectations or demands on one another. Help us to appreciate all that we have as a bonus!

Journal . . .

Week #13

EYES ON THE DOUGHNUT

"Finally, brothers, whatever is true, whatever is noble, whatever is right, whatever is pure, whatever is lovely, whatever is admirable—if anything is excellent or praiseworthy—think about such things."—Philippians 4:8

The apostle Paul gives us the secret to maintaining a positive mental attitude in this passage. The truth is that there are positive and negative aspects of every marriage. This is something we all have in common. We all have certain blessings, gifts and things that God has done in our marriages and homes, and we all have problems, flaws and things that God hasn't done for us in our marriages and homes. That's not the issue. The issue is, "Where do we spend our mental time? Do we dwell on the things that God has done for us, or on the things that God hasn't done for us?" That is the issue. That's the difference between having joy and peace or being miserable the rest of your life. Where are you mentally dwelling? What is your mental address? I'm not saying we shouldn't acknowledge the negatives. That's just as dangerous. We need to bring them into the light and deal with them appropriately. But don't live in the negatives. Find whatever is good, whatever is right, whatever is praiseworthy, and magnify that, and guess what. You'll have more! The bottom line is that whatever you're dwelling on will reproduce itself in reality whether it's positive or negative. So you may as well work on reproducing the positives. As a famous philosopher once said, "As you travel through life's journey, no matter what the goal, keep your eye on the doughnut, and not on the hole." The doughnut represents the substance of what we have. The hole represents what we don't have. Keep your eye on the doughnut.

Question for both of us: What is good and right and admirable in our marriage and home? How can we remind each other to keep our eyes on the doughnut and not on the hole?

Prayer for both of us: Lord, help us to remember that You brought us together for a good and noble purpose. Help us to remember our blessings and the gifts You have given us. Help us keep our eyes on the doughnut and not on the hole.

Journal . . .

Week # 14

FEELINGS

"Be completely humble and gentle; be patient, bearing with one another in love."—Ephesians 4:2

Relationships are built on feelings, not facts. Sometimes a couple will come into our counseling room, and one spouse will begin to share feelings of loneliness, or feelings that the other spouse just doesn't care. About that time I'll look over to the other spouse, and often I'll see a rolling of the eyes, and a tipping back of the head. I wish I had a "thought recorder" capable of playing back thoughts at that moment. I think it would sound like, "Here we go again; of course I care. If I didn't care I wouldn't be here in the first place." Or if the other spouse speaks they might say something like, "Come on, you shouldn't feel that way. Of course I care." In either case we're missing the point that the fact that one might think they really care is totally irrelevant. The issue isn't whether you care or not, it's whether or not your spouse "feels" like you care. It's all about feelings. Throw the facts out the window. They will just confuse the issue. When it comes to relationships we need to zero in on feelings, not facts or circumstances, or even truth (as we see it). This is usually more difficult for men since men think first, then feel. Women tend to feel first, and then think. Ask your typical male how he feels about something, and he'll look back at you with that blank stare that says, "What are you talking about?" The key is to ask him what he "thinks" about something first, then you can ask him how he feels about it. You see, he needs to have the thought first. That provides the place to hang his feelings on. Ask a woman how she feels first, and then she'll be able to share what she thinks about it.

Doing all the right things won't meet the needs of the relationship if one spouse doesn't feel loved, and cared for by the attitude of the heart displayed in the tone of voice and body language of the other spouse. It's all about feelings.

Question for both of us: What things do we do or say that cause the other one to feel unloved or uncared for? What do we tend to communicate with our body language or with our tone of voice? Do we come across as being annoyed, frustrated, or do we just blow it off discounting one another with the way we react? How do we "feel" when we're with each other?

Prayer for both of us: Lord, help us to be humble and gentle with one another. Help us to communicate with words, as well as non-verbal communication, that we really love and care for our spouse. Help us zero in on "feelings."

Journal . . .

Week 15

FIG LEAVES DON'T COVER

"When the woman saw that the fruit of the tree was good for food and pleasing to the eye, and also desirable for gaining wisdom, she took some and ate it. She also gave some to her husband, who was with her, and he ate it. Then the eyes of both of them were opened, and they realized they were naked; so they sewed fig leaves together and made coverings for themselves."—Genesis 3:6, 7

I guess this was the first "cover up". Adam and Eve messed up and they knew it. They felt guilt and shame. So what did they do? They tried to cover their shame with fig leaves. For a while they thought it would work, but it didn't. So they tried to hide from God. That didn't work either. Have things changed much since then? I don't think so. We're still trying to cover up our sin and misdeeds with fig leaves of one kind or another. Perhaps we won't tell the whole truth. Maybe we'll try to compensate for our sin one way or another. Often single parents will give their children everything they want to make up for the absence of the other spouse. I knew of a man who had an affair, but each time he saw his mistress he would be sure to bring home flowers to his wife to cover his own guilt and shame. What a fig leaf! Others use alcohol or drugs to cover the shame. Anger makes for a good fig leaf. I'll get angry enough with others first, so they won't dare ask me about my sin. We've even learned how to use more noble fig leaves like pouring ourselves into our work. It doesn't matter; a fig leaf is a fig leaf. It will never cover, and so you continue to hide from God.

What's the answer then? That hasn't changed either: "The Lord God made garments of skin for Adam and his wife and he clothed them" (Gen. 3:21). For Adam and Eve to be adequately clothed there had to be a sacrifice, the shedding of blood, for the garment of skin to clothe them. And so it is with us. For God to adequately clothe us in a garment of skin we must first "walk in the light (be honest with God and with one another) as he is in the light, and the blood of Jesus cleanses us of all sin (It doesn't just cover it. It washes it away) and we have fellowship one with another" (1 John 1:7). God tells us in His Word that without the shedding of blood there can be no forgiveness. That's why our fig leaves, no matter how noble, will never work. It's only the blood of Jesus that can help us walk in the light, free and forgiven. It allows us to walk in fellowship with our God, and with one another. Let's chuck the fig leaves. Let's put on Christ!

Question for both of us: What are some of the fig leaves we've tried to use to cover up our shortcomings, our insensitivities, and our sin?

Prayer for both of us: Lord, help us to quit the cover up once and for all. It's obvious our fig leaves don't work. Help us to be open and honest with You and with one another, to confess our sin, put on Christ and follow Him all the days of our lives.

Journal . . .

Week #16

FIX THE PROBLEM!

"By wisdom a house is built, and through understanding it is established; through knowledge its rooms are filled with rare and beautiful treasures."—Proverbs 24:3, 4

If I had called an electrician to come fix our dishwasher, and if that electrician didn't have the skill to fix the dishwasher, but instead took it upon himself to go about fixing the toaster, a lamp, and an electrical outlet, and then presented me with a bill for three hours of work (while the dishwasher was still broke), should I pay him? Couldn't he argue that he did so much work, and after all, he did fix things that he thought should be fixed? But he didn't fix what you called him for! The dishwasher is still broke! He may feel like he did a lot of work, and in fact, he did, but he didn't fix what was broke. Therefore no payment!

Well, it's no different with marriage. When there's a problem no amount of work in other areas will bring us the reward we seek until we fix the problem. A husband could buy all the gifts in the world for his wife, but if what she needs is time with him, he's just wasting his money building a false sense of security in thinking that what he's doing will compensate for what he hasn't fixed. Forget it. It won't work. A wife who's not sexually available for her husband shouldn't be lulled into thinking that a clean house will make up for a lack of sex. It won't happen.

Those other things are good. Don't get me wrong. We should be buying gifts and keeping a clean house, but don't for a minute think they will compensate for whatever is broke in the marriage. You're wasting your energy if you think you can make it work. It won't. You might feel like you're working on your marriage, like the ill trained electrician certainly felt he was putting in a good day's work, but it's only wasted energy if you're not fixing what's broke.

Identify the problem, and start working on it. If you don't know how, don't go to something you know how to do. The marriage will still be broke. Learn. Pull out the books. Talk about it. Don't stop until you've addressed the problem, and fix the "dishwasher." Then you can look for payment. It will be there, for sure!

Question for both of us: What are some of the things that are broke in our marriage? How have we tried to compensate by trying to work on other areas that we feel more confident about? What has been the result?

Prayer for both of us: Lord, help us to identify what the real problems are and do whatever it takes to learn how to fix them. Keep us from being deceived, and lulled into a false sense of security because we think we're working so hard doing the wrong things. Help us to fix the problem.

Journal . . .

Week #17

FORGIVENESS AND FORGIVINGNESS

"Bear with each other and forgive whatever grievances you may have against one another. Forgive as the Lord has forgiven you."—Colossians 3:13

It becomes much easier to forgive one another when we understand how the "flow" of forgiveness works, or "the flow of grace." Forgiveness is a dynamic thing that must always be moving to be effective. The source of forgiveness is God. From Him we receive forgiveness for our many sins, past, present and future. He releases His grace to flood our souls with forgiveness. (This was made possible only through the death and resurrection of Christ 2000 years ago.) As we receive forgiveness the flow of grace cleanses us and makes us clean. Then, however, the flow must continue as we are forgiving others, even as they are trespassing against us. The flow must be uninterrupted—forgiveness received while we are, in fact, forgiving others, like a river flowing cleansing all in its path.

If I stop the flow of grace by refusing to forgive my spouse, or anyone else, the river stops. The flow is halted. In time, the water begins to grow murky as bacteria and germs begin to grow in the still, motionless water. In the same way, bitterness and anger begin to grow in my spirit if I stop the flow of grace. It becomes a bitter pool. I must let the living waters of grace flow by forgiving others even as I have been forgiven. The problem is that we often don't want to see our spouses "get away with it" or "get off too easy." Don't worry about it. Forgiving your spouse doesn't get them forgiven. Each one must present themselves, personally, to the throne of grace. Personal repentance is the only way one can receive true forgiveness. The only thing forgiving others really does is to release them to God for judgment instead of carrying the judgment in your own spirit. It also restores relationship. So, it's really for your own benefit that you must keep the flow moving by forgiving even as you have been forgiven. God cannot pour more forgiveness into a bitter pool backing up with unforgiveness and resentment. He can only pour it into a clear flowing stream. That's why Jesus taught that you cannot be forgiven unless you are forgiving.

Question for both of us: How is the flow of grace doing in our marriage? Is the river flowing? Where is it stopped up?

Prayer for both of us: Lord, help us to live in a state of forgiveness and forgivingness. Help us to keep the river of grace moving in our lives and marriage. Help us to forgive each other so that You may forgive us.

Journal . . .

FREEDOM!

"It is for freedom that Christ has set us free. Stand firm then, and do not let yourselves be burdened again by a yoke of slavery."—Galatians 5:1

Freedom is a wonderful thing—if we understand what it means. Whether we speak of national freedom or personal freedom the principles are the same. Yet today marriages and relationships are in turmoil. This is reflected in a national decline of civility and order. As the church goes, so goes the family; as the family goes, so goes the nation. Freedom is never absolute. It is bounded by the will and purposes of God. Freedom is to know that I am personally accepted and loved by the Supreme Judge of the universe who created me in His image. Therefore, I'm not in need of the approval of others. I am free to be who He made me to be, fully and completely.

Freedom is knowing that our marriage is divinely ordained. As we walk in the light sharing our thoughts, feelings and actions, holding ourselves mutually accountable to God and His laws, we come to know, and accept one another for who we are. Freedom is knowing that I am free to pass on to my children a legacy of faith, hope and love. The next generation will be deeply impacted by choices we make—or fail to make—even as we are deeply impacted by the choices our parents made.

Ultimate freedom is the freedom to follow Christ. Outside of Christ there is only bondage, seen or unseen, which results in misery in this life, and an eternity separated from the God who made us. It is for freedom that Christ has set us free.

Therefore let us freely pursue His will, and the joy promised will be more than just words in a book. It will be real in our lives, in our marriage, in our family and in our nation.

Question for both of us: Do we really value and exercise our freedoms to be the very best we can, or are we still in bondage to people, circumstances, or attitudes?

Prayer for both of us: Lord, help us to know the freedom that sets us free to soar to new heights in love, mercy, and yes, even righteousness. Become all that we need that we might be free to be who You called us to be. Help us to be good stewards of the freedom You purchased for us on a hill called Golgotha.

Journal . . .

FRUIT INSPECTORS

"But the fruit of the Spirit is love, joy, peace, patience, kindness, goodness, faithfulness, gentleness and self-control. Against such things there is no law."—Galatians 5:22, 23

My heart breaks each time I meet a believer who has known the Lord for a significant amount of time, and is still struggling with the same issues they struggled with before he or she same to know Christ. What happened in those years? Has there been no growth? Being born again is just the beginning. A newborn baby doesn't stay newborn. He grows. Yet, I'm sorry to say that many who are newly born into the Kingdom of God remain newborns. They simply don't grow. How can we tell how much we're growing? Don't go by how well one knows the Bible, or how active one is in church. That's no measure of Christian character. That only measures one's religiosity. Spiritual growth can only be adequately measured by the fruit of God's Spirit that is evident in one's life. That's the true test.

Take a look at each of the listed fruit and rate yourself on a scale of 1 to 10 (1 being the least, 10 meaning you've arrived). How much of each of the Spirit's fruit is evident in your life? Take inventory. Then do the same for your spouse. Then sit down together and switch papers and dialogue on the subject. Then do it again next year, and the next, and the next, until Jesus comes for the harvest.

Questions for both of us: What fruit of the Spirit is God trying to develop in me this year, in particular? What fruit is he trying to develop in my spouse?

Prayer for both of us: Lord, help us to remain under the hand of the Vinedresser, as You prune us, and work in us to develop a harvest of fruit. Help us to increase in our fruit day-by-day, week-by-week, month-by-month, year-by-year, that others might see in us the fruit of Your Spirit, and that we would bring honor to Your name.

Journal . . .

Week #20

GIVING FREELY

"Each one should give what he has decided in his heart to give, not reluctantly or under compulsion, for God loves a cheerful giver"—2 Corinthians 9:7

John was upset because his wife, Mary, wouldn't give him more sex. After expressing his anger every way he could, John convinced Mary that she wasn't being a good Christian wife. Mary began to give him more sex, but it just didn't satisfy. Why? Because Mary was doing it out of obedience, compulsion, and a sense of obligation. Now John resented the fact that she "just wasn't into it." The truth is that John had her body but he didn't have her heart, and that was what he really desired. Every man wants to be desired. Sex is an expression of desire. If there is no desire sex becomes a mechanical ritual, through which both parties come to resent each other. What then is the answer to this timeless problem? John has to change his focus from the physical to the emotional. He has to set out to win Mary's heart again, and do whatever it will take to help her feel loved and cared for. The natural response will be a desire for relationship, which finds expression in a true heartfelt desire for sex. Then the giving of oneself will be body, soul and spirit. She will want to have more sex because God will put it in her heart to give, and it will be genuine. John may continue to demand the physical act only and also continue in his frustration and feelings of inadequacy, or he can work to meet Mary's emotional needs, and wait until God puts it in her heart to give, freely and unconditionally, simply because she loves and desires him. It may involve a waiting period, but it's more than worth the wait to receive not just sex, but love in all its fullness.

Question for both of us: Do we have sex, or anything else, because God has placed it in our hearts to freely give, or are we giving because we feel compelled, and the truth is we really resent it?

Prayer for both of us: Lord, change our hearts that we would be willing to forego those things that are given out of a sense of obligation or compulsion in order to wait until they are given unconditionally from a sincere heart. Help us to win the hearts of our mates.

Journal . . .

GOD IS IN CONTROL

"Then I heard what sounded like a great multitude, like the roar of rushing waters and like loud peals of thunder, shouting: Hallelujah! For our Lord God Almighty reigns."
—Revelation 19:6

The older we get the more Penny and I realize that we tend to live our lives, not according to some deep philosophy of life, but by simple one-liners, like "God is in control." (Therefore, we don't have to be.) I remember when we were going through some of our most difficult times, how Penny would simply take a deep breath and declare, "God is in control." With that declaration we could then go on. You see, there's a sense of comfort in knowing that God is in control, and he won't let anything happen that isn't in our best interest, even when we can't see it. He is the God of the unknown, and because I know the God of the unknown is a good God I can be at rest. I can let go. I may not understand everything that's happening. I may not like it. But I can rest in knowing that God will work all things together for my good if I will simply love Him and remain available for His purposes (Romans 8:28). When I feel like things are getting out of control I don't have to grasp for control and add to the confusion. I can let go because I know my God, who never even sleeps, is on the job. He is in control, and He won't let anything happen to me that isn't for my own good. He loves me. God is in control, so I don't have to be. I remember one individual who made up little signs and posted them all over her house to remind her that "God is in control." That just might be a good idea to remind us that The Lord Almighty reigns—God is in control, and He's a good God who won't let anything happen to me that

50

isn't for my own good. I can let go, because I know that He doesn't.

Question for both of us: When do we tend to panic and grasp for control? What can we do to help remind each other that God is in control, therefore we don't have to be?

Prayer for both of us: Lord, help us to abide in You, to know in our hearts, not just our heads, that You really are in control, therefore we don't have to be. Help us to let go, to trust, to rest in You.

Journal . . .

Week #22

GROWING IN ONENESS

"For he himself is our peace, who has made the two one and has destroyed the barrier, the dividing wall of hostility. . . . speaking the truth in love, we will in all things grow up into him, who is the head."—Ephesians 2:14; 4:15

Though, Paul was speaking specifically about the dividing wall between the Jews and the Gentiles, the principle remains true for all relationships where dividing walls have been erected, most immediately, of course, the dividing walls between a husband and a wife. We need to be honest with ourselves. Have we really surrendered our own self-wills to the will of God in our marriage? Have we really traded in our different positions for the same purpose—His purpose? That's the only way the oneness can be achieved. Oneness is not the absorption of one personality into the personality of the other. Oneness is found when both are surrendered to conforming to God's will, so that it's no longer "my way" or "your way," but it becomes "His way."

Our struggle is not to convince our spouse to our way of thinking. Our struggle is for both of us to work together to find God's way of thinking in a given matter. Paul tells us how to do this. ". . . Speaking the truth in love, we will in all things grow up into him. . . ." To find that oneness centered in Christ we must be free to speak the truth in love without fear of rejection or judgment, and without trying to dominate our partner's will and thought patterns. No matter how uncomfortable, we must be able to share how we truly feel about the matter and have mutual respect for one another's feelings, whether we agree, or understand it, or not. Our struggle is to work to find agreement concerning God's will in the matter, not our own. As we both remain submitted to the process we grow in oneness day by day. No one's identity gets lost, and God remains in the very center of our relationship. After all, it's as Paul said, He is ". . . the head."

Question for both of us: Have we been growing in oneness, with God in the center of our relationship?

Prayer for both of us: Lord, help us to put our self-wills aside. Help us to work together to seek Your will for every aspect of our lives and marriage. Help us be that cord of three strands; You in the center, and both of us wrapped tightly around You. That cord will not easily be broken.

Journal . . .

Week #23

HEAD OF THE HOUSE?

"For he has put everything under his feet. . . . When he has done this, then the Son himself, will be made subject to him who put everything under him, so that God may be all in all."—1 Corinthians 15:27, 28

What does it mean to be the head of the house? Simply put, it means being the head servant. God demonstrated His authority as the Head of Christ by first putting everything under His feet. Then Christ made Himself subject to the Father. That's the sequence. That's the way it happens. First, the husband places everything under the feet of his wife; then she willingly places herself under his authority, because it's safe. I've said it before—I don't know of a single woman who wouldn't gladly place herself under the authority of a man who would first lay the world at her feet. The key word is "first". Now please, I don't mean to give the wife whatever she wants. I certainly don't mean the husband is to be a doormat for the wife. I do mean the husband is to study and know her physical and emotional needs, and he must work to meet those needs. The husband is the initiator, the wife the responder. As the husband first learns to serve his wife, unconditionally, she then begins to feel safe, and begins to place herself under his trustworthy and safe care. It must be a place of security and safety otherwise it won't work. If you have to demand it, then you surely don't have it. Learn to serve, unconditionally, and it will happen out of relationship, rather than compulsion, by grace rather than by law. That's Biblical headship and submission.

Question for both of us: Is submission in our home out of compulsion or out of relationship? How can we work toward realizing the principle revealed in 1 Corinthians 15:27, 28 in our home?

Prayer for both of us: Lord, help us to surrender to Your principle of headship through servanthood. Help Your order of Biblical headship and submission through grace rather than law be real in our marriage.

Journal . . .

Week #24

HONOR ONE ANOTHER

"Love must be sincere. Hate what is evil; cling to what is good. Be devoted to one another in brotherly love. Honor one another above yourselves."—Romans 12:10

Honor. That's not a word we hear too often in modern culture. In fact, with all the millions of dollars spent on Superbowl commercials yesterday, I didn't hear the word "honor," mentioned once. I guess it just doesn't sell. Yet it is the very foundation of a lasting relationship. Without honoring one another there can be no mutual respect. Without mutual respect there can be no intimacy. Without intimacy there is no real relationship.

What does it mean to honor one another? I think it means to acknowledge ones' presence with a sense of awe. How would you respond if the most highly respected person you could think of walked into the room you were in? If you can't think of anyone, how would you respond to Jesus if He walked into the room? You would probably stand up as your mouth dropped open in a sense of awe. Wow! It's really Him! Hold on to that picture. That's the way we want to respond to our spouse as they enter the room we are in. "But he, or she isn't Jesus," you say. Maybe not, but isn't he or she the most important person in the world to you? If that's true, shouldn't there be a sense of awe in their presence? If that's not true, then I think you have some adjustments to make. When we feel honored we feel uplifted. That's what it means to honor one another "above yourselves." When we feel uplifted our basic need for significance or security is met freeing us to respond in a way that allows us to give respect and honor back, because we have first received it. Now both parties are lifting each other up instead of dishonoring one another, and tearing one another down. Let's honor one another by acknowledging one another's presence when they walk into the room, by turning our full attention to them when they begin to talk to us, by greeting them at the door when they come home. Treat one another in the moment-by-moment events of the day like they are the most important person in the world to you. They are. Then remember, "What you do to the least of these brethren you do to me"—Jesus.

Question for both of us: Do we really go out of our way to honor one another, or do we feel dishonored by one another, how?

Prayer for both of us: Lord, help us to see one another as the most important person in this world. Help us to honor one another above ourselves throughout the day, each time our eyes meet, each time we speak to one another. Be glorified, Lord in the way we treat one another. Remind us that in the same way we are also treating You.

Journal . . .

Week #25

INTIMACY OR SEX?

"Now for the matters you wrote about: It is good for a man not to marry. But since there is so much immorality, each man should have his own wife, and each woman her own husband. The husband should fulfill his marital duty to his wife, and likewise the wife to her husband. The wife's body does not belong to her alone but also to her husband. In the same way, the husband's body does not belong to him alone but also to his wife. Do not deprive each other except by mutual consent and for a time, so that you may devote yourselves to prayer. Then come together again so that Satan will not tempt you because of your lack of self-control. I say this as a concession, not as a command."—1 Corinthians 7:1-6

Unfortunately, when I've heard this passage quoted it was usually a husband trying to convince his wife that her body belonged to him, and therefore, she had a Christian duty to give him sex whenever he wanted it. Talk about twisting Scripture! All one has to do is to look closely at this passage to see that Paul was talking about mutual respect, mutual desire and mutual agreement. That's when sex becomes more than sex. It becomes intimacy. Animals have sex. Only God's human creation has the capacity for intimacy, a divine oneness in the sexual experience that grows out of mutual respect, mutual desire and mutual agreement. Granted, it's a lot easier to settle for just sex, but ultimately it leaves one unfulfilled. There's something in us that tells us there's supposed to be more than just a physical release. The wife who is just doing her "wifely duties" by "servicing" her husband whenever he wants it will begin to resent him over time for making her feel used. She eventually loses respect for herself and for him. The walls eventually go up. Intimacy is lost.

True sexual intimacy happens when we have struggled together to find that mutual respect, mutual desire and mutual agreement. Only then is there a chance to become one, not just physically, but emotionally and spiritually, as well. You see, sex is a gift given to us by God to give us a taste of Heaven here on earth. Just as we, who know Christ, will be one with Him one day, God allows us to experience a taste of that oneness here on earth with our spouse. When we've been able to communicate and have "fellowship" with each other, and truly sense there is mutual respect, desire and agreement, then sex is the icing on the cake. It's as close to heaven as we'll get this side of glory. When we don't have the "fellowship" sex becomes an increasingly unfulfilling experience, because what we crave—the intimacy—is absent. Let's strive together, even struggle together, to come to that mutual respect, desire and agreement. Then sex will be beyond all we can ask or imagine.

Question for both of us: Do we really enjoy the gift God has given us in sexual intimacy, or do we just have sex with resentment? Do we feel we have mutual respect, mutual desires and mutual agreement when it comes to how we make love?

Prayer for both of us: Lord, help us to do whatever it will take to build mutual respect, to discuss our desires, and to work toward mutual agreement so that we will enjoy the gift of sex without resentment and bitterness. We want only Your love manifested in our relationship.

Journal . . .

Week #26

IT'S ALL HIS, ANYWAY

"The earth is the Lord's, and everything in it, the world, and all who live in it."—Psalm 24:1

I often think about that day when I will stand before God, and hear Him say, "Well Bill, how did you do with that ministry I entrusted to you? How did you do with the house, car and all the other things I let you use? Oh, and let's not forget the most important things I entrusted to you: How did you do with that marriage and family I let you manage?" I realize this will be no time for excuses. The Master trusted me to care for these people and things for Him. I will have to answer to Him. I guess it's only natural that I tend to care for things that don't belong to me better than I care for my own things. If I borrow something from a neighbor—say a lawnmower—I'm much more careful because I know it doesn't belong to me. If I break it, not only will the tool have to be replaced, but I will have lost my friend's trust as well. He thought enough of me to trust me with his lawnmower. The least I could do is live up to that trust.

First we must remind ourselves that none of it belongs to us. It all belongs to God—everything and everyone. He has thought enough of us to entrust us with jobs, homes, finances, and most importantly, our children and our husbands and wives. Are we living up to that trust, or just treating things as though they belonged to us? You know the attitude; "It's my job; if I want to blow it I will." "It's my house; if I want to keep it a mess I can." "They're my children. I'll raise them how I want." "It's my marriage; if I want to end it, that's my decision." Well, these might reflect the general attitudes of this world. But they're wrong. None of it is ours. Therefore, we don't have the right to do what we want, or even what we think is best. We have a responsibility to the Owner to take care of His property according to His wishes.

If He can't trust us to care for His property, and the people he has already given us, don't think He'll entrust us with more. God is no fool.

Question for both of us: Do we tend to take care of someone else's property better than our own? Do we take care of everything God has entrusted us with like it belongs to Him? If we stood before God today how would we answer God when He asked us about all He had entrusted us with, especially our relationships?

Prayer for both of us: Lord, help us to remember that it all belongs to You. Help us to take care of all that You have entrusted us with, especially our children and each other in such a way that You will be pleased.

Journal . . .

LOVE COMPELS—SIN REPELS

"For Christ's love compels us, because we are convinced that one died for all, and therefore all died. And he died for all, that those who live should no longer live for themselves but for him who died for them and was raised again.
—1 Corinthians 15:14, 15

The quality of our most important relationships is really a function of the small decisions we make, like "Shall I ask her how her day was, or just go turn on the T.V. to relax?" "Do I quit what I'm doing long enough to go meet him at the door when I hear the car pull up?" We are naturally self-centered, and inclined to do what's easiest for us. That's not love. Love is a compelling force that moves us toward seeking one another's best interest, preferring one another over ourselves. Sin is a repelling force that causes us to withdraw into seeking our own comfort or protection. I may not want to ask my wife how her day went, perhaps because I really don't care right now. I'm tired. I worked all day. I just want to plop my feet up on the hassock and chill. The wife may not want to cut her phone conversation short with her best friend when she hears hubby's car pull up. After all, she hasn't talked to her all week, and there's much to catch up on. If we're going to love each other we need to let Christ's love compel us toward one another precisely when it means sacrifice. There is no love without sacrifice. In fact, love without sacrifice is useless. Furthermore, we must be compelled to love even when it means risking conflict. Yes, working through conflict is part of love. It's Christ's love that compels us to do whatever it takes to draw closer in oneness, even when it means dealing with conflict. It's sin that repels us from one another. Even when we say "I'll let him/her have their own way. I don't want to start a fight," and we just go off in a huff; if we find ourselves being repelled, for whatever reason, know it's not love. It's sin. Sin repels; love compels.

Question for both of us: When do I tend to pull away from you? When do I feel you tend to pull away from me? How can we sincerely let Christ's love compel us when we naturally don't feel like engaging?

Prayer for both of us: Lord, help us to remember that it was Your love for us that compelled You to die that we might know love. You didn't live for Yourself, but for us. Help us, in the same way, to choose to not live for ourselves but for You. Compelled by Your love, help us to love one another, that in our relationship the world will see Jesus.

Journal . . .

Week #28

OH HOLY VACATION!

"Six days do your work, but on the seventh day do not work, so that your ox and your donkey may rest and the slave born in your household, and the alien as well, may be refreshed."
—Exodus 23:12

I remember when I used to feel guilty if I took time off for vacation, especially during those early years when I was planting a church, or shepherding a congregation. There was always so much work to do! Our society seems to place such a high value on "busyness." Well, we just returned from a week in a cabin on a lake where all we did was rest, fish, play Scrabble, fuss over Nikki (our pooch), make love and enjoy each other. It was great! It was more than that. It was holy! Throughout Scripture the Sabbath principle reminds us that it is nothing less than God's instruction to take time on a regular basis to rest and be renewed and re-energized in order to serve God, and others more effectively. No one is at their best when they're burned out. One gets irritable, frustrated and angry when they haven't had the time to rest. It happens to us too. We spend so much time helping others with their marriages that, we, too, need time to enjoy the marriage God has given us. We, too, need time just to enjoy each other, to rest in one another's arms without having to think of the things that need to be done, or the people who need to be called, or the bills that need to be paid.

The best thing we can do for God, and for those whom we serve in ministry, is to be renewed and refreshed, by taking time off for a "holy-day," a vacation. Perhaps it would do us well in this society of "human doings" (instead of human beings), to write a church hymn that went like "O Holy Vacation. . . . The lake is clearly calling. . . ." You get the idea.

Make a "holiday" (which derives from the words "holy day") a priority for your marriage. Make the time to be together and enjoy the gift of marriage. Discipline yourself to obey God's instruction for a productive and balanced life. It's the best thing you can do for God, and for those whom He has placed under your very own ministry. Yep, that's right, "your ministry."

Question for both of us: Do we really take enough time on a regular basis to enjoy one another, and be renewed and refreshed so that we can serve God and others more effectively?

Prayer for both of us: Lord, help us to be disciplined enough to make the time we need to enjoy this gift of marriage You've given us, to be renewed and refreshed, and most of all, to enjoy Your presence anew in our lives. Help us to have a "holy-day" worth singing about.

Journal . . .

Week #29

MARRIAGE TRAINING?

"Have nothing to do with godless myths and old wives' tales; rather, train yourself to be godly. For physical training is of some value, but godliness has value for all things, holding promise for both the present life and the life to come."
—1 Timothy 4:7, 8

Who would ever think of such a thing as marriage training? That's ridiculous! Is it really? Why are so many marriages failing? Why are so many couples unable to communicate and live in true partnership when that's really what they both want? They simply haven't been trained, so they just don't have the ability to do it. Training is not learning. Don't get them confused. An athlete can know how to excel in his sport. He can have all the right information stored in his memory banks, but if he has not trained himself in a purposeful, diligent way, he simply will not have the ability to apply the knowledge he has. Just as an athlete must assess his weak areas, and go on a program to strengthen him in those areas until they are developed, so too, we must assess our marriages, identify the weak areas, and put ourselves on a program to build them up. It's not enough to just read another book, or attend another seminar. We must go into training. First, find a coach who will hold you accountable. It could be your spouse, a friend, a pastor or a counselor. Make sure it's someone who will love you enough to tell you the truth even when you don't want to hear it. Then assess the strengths and weaknesses of your marriage. Identify the weaknesses, and start doing whatever it takes to train yourself to develop your relationship muscles to build a strong marriage. It's a process. It's fantasy to think it will just happen. What athlete would go to competition and expect to win without training? And it will be work. You know how the saying goes, "No pain, no gain." It's just the same when we're training ourselves to be the spouse God has called us to be. Keep your eye on the prize: a marriage that will bring fulfillment and love to each of you, present the model that your children need to see, and ultimately, reflect the glory and the grace of God to a world without hope. That's the "gold." As difficult as the training may become, it's just so worth it!!

Question for both of us: Are we really in training to build a marriage that will win? Who do we know who may be willing to be our coach? What areas need work?

Prayer for both of us: Lord, help us to take the need for marriage training seriously. Help us to commit to a program to work out, and keep working out, until we build up those areas that are weak. Help us to be committed as good athletes and win the race by crossing the finish line together for this life, and the life to come.

Journal . . .

Week #30

NO JESUS, NO PEACE

"If you, even you had only known on this day what would bring you peace—but now it is hidden from your eyes."
—Jesus, Luke 19:42

We have more technological advancements, more knowledge, more resources, more wealth, more of everything, and less of the thing that matters most—peace, real peace. Everybody's running this way and that. Now that we have computers we even have more time to run more places, and do more things. Jesus looked over Jerusalem, and the Bible tells us He wept over what He saw: people who were running every which way, because they couldn't see what would bring them real peace. He wept because He saw into their future. He knew they were setting themselves up for a life of defeat because they didn't recognize that the Prince of Peace was among them. They were too busy. How sad!

Has anything really changed? I don't think so. Human nature is as changeable as a leopard's spots. I believe Jesus is still weeping over us today, because we're too busy to recognize that He is among us. What really brings peace is nothing other than the Prince of Peace, Himself. Perhaps you've seen the bumper sticker: "No Jesus—No Peace"

If our marriages and relationships are not centered in Christ, there will be no peace. No Jesus—No Peace. Get as busy as you like. Work as much as you can. You'll still find no peace outside of Christ. Think about it.

Question for dialogue: When do we feel most peaceful? How have we not recognized the presence of Christ in our lives? How can we change that for the better?

Prayer for both of us: Lord, help us to acknowledge Your presence in our lives. Open the eyes of our hearts that we might see You among us, and know what will truly bring us peace.

Journal . . .

TIMES OF REFRESHING

"Repent, then, and turn to God, so that your sins may be wiped out, that the times of refreshing may come from The Lord, and that he may send the Christ who has been appointed for you—even Jesus."—Acts 3:19

I felt led to write about "the times of refreshing" since Penny and I just returned from a much needed week's vacation on the Jersey Shore, a much needed time of refreshing. I was thinking about being refreshed so I turned to the third chapter of Acts where I remembered Peter spoke about the subject, and there it was, big as life: *REPENT . . . then turn to God . . . that the times of refreshing may come.* Who wants to hear that? But nevertheless, there's no way around it. In fact, that is the very key to experiencing the times of refreshing. We need to be able to stand before God, drop our fig leaves, and be open and honest with God and one another that the refreshing winds of The Holy Spirit can blow over us and into every part of our lives. We need to repent and be honest not just about our actions but also about our opinions, feelings and thoughts. Of course, we need to use wisdom on timing and substance concerning what and how we share, but we need to share, honestly. If our actions, thoughts or opinions are not pleasing to God, then we need to get on our knees and ask God to change our hearts, make us new. God is looking for the heart that is, first of all, honest then desiring to change to be pleasing to Him. The only sin God cannot forgive is the one we don't confess to Him. So, let's quit justifying, rationalizing or minimizing our sin. Let's call it for what it is. Let's repent, and enjoy the times of refreshing that God, so much, wants us to experience.

Question to ask each other for dialogue: What persistent sin do you see in me that you believe keeps me from experiencing the refreshing winds of the Holy Spirit? (Answer truthfully yet lovingly?)

Prayer for both of us: "Lord, help us to be courageous enough to walk in truth. Help us to see those areas that are not pleasing to You that we may truly repent, and begin to change. Help us experience the refreshing winds of Your Spirit together as a couple whom you have joined together forever."

Journal . . .

RELATIONSHIPS OR VOLLEYBALLS?

"Love must be sincere. Hate what is evil; cling to what is good. Be devoted to one another in brotherly love. Honor one another above yourselves."—Romans 12:9, 10

In the Tom Hanks movie "Castaway," a business executive who lives for his work finds himself alone on a desert island with only a volleyball to talk to. I thought it interesting that there was absolutely no mention of God in a situation where one would reasonably expect even an agnostic to be found challenging God to prove He existed by coming to his aid. But it seems like Hollywood is either too far gone to think about God, or purposely avoided mention of God to prevent the audience from thinking that there just might be a God who can help in these situations. In either case, the story serves to illustrate that what really is important in life is "relation-ships." That's what really matters. Relationships are precious. When unforeseen circumstances cause us to lose relationships it's sad. When, by our own actions, we fail to provide the time and energy needed to maintain and build our relationships, that's foolishness. The real question is, "Will we have more than a volleyball to relate with?" Have we spent time building relationship with God, building relationship with one another, building intimacy? You know, "into-me-see." That takes time and focus, not talking about the job, or the children, or the house, but focus on one another's feelings and needs. The most punishing enemy of the human soul is loneliness. It's easy to be lonely in a crowded room. It's easy to live in a house filled with lonely people, all under the same roof. It's also sad. Everyone's busy with their own lives, but no one is building a life in common. No intimacy. What will you have down the road in a few years, meaningful relationships, or a volleyball?

Question for both of us: What time do we spend together sharing our feelings and our needs, building intimacy, saying to one another, "Into me see?" Are we afraid to? Why? What can we do to devote time to building relationships?

Prayer for both of us: Lord, help us to rearrange our lives and priorities so that we will invest time and energy into building and maintaining deep and meaningful relationships with one another, then with others. Help us disengage from the "rat race." Help us engage in "the good race."

Journal . . .

WHAT ARE VACATIONS FOR?

"Love the LORD your God with all your heart and with all your soul and with all your strength. These commandments that I give you today are to be upon your hearts. Impress them on your children. Talk about them when you sit at home and when you walk along the road, when you lie down and when you get up. Tie them as symbols on your hands and bind them on your foreheads. Write them on the doorframes of your houses and on your gates."—Deuteronomy 6:5-9...

Summer vacations. This is a time to re-connect, rediscover, and rededicate. First we need to reconnect with our Maker. Get out in the woods, on the lake, ponder the mighty seas, but gaze on His magnificent creation and look for the hands and the heart that have created such beauty. And say again, "I will love the Lord with all my heart, and all my soul and all my strength." That means He's number one. He won't take second place. As the song goes, if He isn't Lord of all, then He's not Lord at all, He won't play second fiddle. Secondly, rediscover God's will concerning you. Get into His Word like never before. Now that the children are home, bored, use this time to teach the children, not just in a formal family devotional setting, but when you're with them on the beach. Tell them how God promised Abraham that His descendants would be as the grains of sand on the shore. If you're not sure where to look, and you're in the woods, look up "trees" and you can teach your children how the "trees" of the fields clap their hands in praise of God, and how the mountains will "bow down" and the seas will "roar" at the sound of His name. There's so much that a good family vacation can tell about our God as we set to rediscover Him. Then let's rededicate ourselves as a family, first to God, then to one another. Here it's up to Dad to provide that loving leadership (no tyrants allowed). Let Dad be the "first servant" and his family will follow. Whether it's around a campfire, at a poolside, or on the shore, we can all gather and thank God for this time of refreshing and rest, and rededicate ourselves to Him, and His purposes for our lives. Let's give ourselves to being more faithful, more obedient, more a servant. Let's commit our home to being a place where "each lives for the other, and all live for God." Let's reconnect, rediscover and rededicate. That will be the best part of your whole vacation.

Question for both of us: When was the last time we rededicated ourselves, our family and our home to the Lord and His purposes? How can we schedule a vacation, and include God in our plans?

Prayer for both of us: Lord, help us to have a time of rest and refreshing where we can reconnect with You, rediscover Your will for our marriage and family, and rededicate our family to Your purposes.

Journal . . .

REPENTANCE?—UGH!

"From that time on Jesus began to preach, 'Repent, for the Kingdom of Heaven is near.' "—Matthew 4:17

Repentance? That's not exactly a word that brings warm fuzzies. Who needs it? Can't we just talk about God's love for all of us, and how we will all go to heaven if we just mean well? Sorry! Jesus' first message was not "God loves you." It was "Repent!" The truth is that we can't know God's love without first repenting; changing our ways, turning from what we think is right to what He says is right. Then, to the extent that we can practice repentance, we can know His love in greater measure. Our sin occupies space that His love seeks to displace. When a client asks me how they can hear God's voice my standard answer is, "Ask Him to tell you what your sins are, and I'll bet you'll hear Him." You know what? It works every time. As God reveals your sin make a list and begin choosing to change your mind about your sin, and pray for the power to change. God will provide the power, but He leaves the choice up to you. If you don't make the choice, He can't provide the power. I've seen lives change dramatically at the altar, but I've seen more lives change day by day, sin by sin, repentance by repentance. The good news is that every act of true repentance opens us to enjoy more of God's love. Don't get me wrong. His love is always there, but it's our ability to receive it that is hindered by our sin. Be bold and courageous. Choose to repent. Turn from your "wicked" ways. Turn to God's ways. Make a list of the sin that God reveals to you when you ask Him in prayer. Then choose to change one by one, little by little, and know more love as you go—as you grow. The alternative is nothing less than missing heaven and knowing hell. There's no in-between. Sorry!

Question for both of us: How often do we really take inventory of our own sin? Do we talk about our own sin, or just point the finger at each other?

Prayer for both of us: Lord, help us to take an honest inventory of our own sin, and hold ourselves accountable to each other as we begin to change our ways sin by sin, that we might enjoy more and more of Your love for us. Help us to repent, for the Kingdom of Heaven is truly at hand.

Journal . . .

Week #35

RESPOND VS. REACTING

"Set a guard over my mouth, O Lord; keep watch over the door of my lips."—Psalm 141:3

What kind of a prayer is that? Unfortunately, it's probably a prayer that most of us need to be praying more often. Too often we blurt out things that we wish we could take back. Sometimes, even as they are leaving our mouths we wish somehow they could make a U-turn and come back into our mouths before they go out and kill. Don't feel bad. It's natural. But just because it's natural that doesn't mean it's good. If you stand in front of me while I cross my legs and tap my knee with a small rubber mallet, you're going to get kicked by my very natural reflex. That's what we do to each other when we just blurt out what's natural. But wait a minute. Didn't God make us a little higher than the animals? Didn't He give us a brain so we could choose our responses instead of going with our natural reflex like any baboon? He sure did! That's why we can choose to respond instead of naturally reacting. But it will take using the brain God gave us. Could it be that too often we just don't?

Next time your husband or your wife tries to test your reflexes pay attention to that guard God has set over your mouth, and hold back from what your reflexes would say. Stop. Think. Then let the words that come out of your mouth be a product of an intelligently thought out response instead of a baboon reflex. *Respond instead of reacting.*

Question for both of us: How do I let you push my buttons that causes me to react without thinking? How do I push yours?

78

Prayer for both of us: Lord, help us to learn to respond instead of reacting so that our marriage will be a product of an intelligently thought out plan instead of a product of our natural base instincts.

Journal . . .

Week #36

SETTING THE EXAMPLE

Follow my example, as I follow the example of Christ.
—1 Corinthians 11:1

Your children will be like you. They are catching whatever it is you have, the good and the bad. They are following the example you are setting, for better or worse. Your co-workers, your friends, your other family members are all allowing some of you to rub off on them. You are leading by example whether you intend to or not. The question is to where are you leading your children and those in your sphere of influence? Are you leading them up, or are you leading them down? We just attended the 70th birthday party of a well known religious leader, during which time each of his children, now grown with families of their own, stood up and spoke of their dad. The one thing that impressed me, and brought some conviction to my own heart, was how each one said that what they remembered most was how every morning, when they woke up, their dad could always be found in his den with his Bible on his knees in prayer. What an example! Though prayer had always been a regular part of my life, I was not quite that public with it, or as regular. Though I pray continually, my children didn't see it most of the time. I didn't set the example. I can't change the past. I can only ask God's forgiveness for my shortcomings as a Christian, as a husband, and as a father, and go from here purposed in my heart to set the example; to lead my family up, not down; to become the person I want my children (now grown) to be. His blessings are new every morning, and great is His faithfulness. I'm confident that He who began a good work in me will complete it.

Question for the both of Us: What kind of an example have we set for our children and those in our sphere of influence?

80

Are we the kind of people we want our children to become? What changes can we make?

Prayer for both of us: Lord, forgive us for not setting the right example. Help us to change. Help us to be the example that will reflect Your nature and Your character to our children and those around us.

Journal . . .

THE FEAR OF CHRIST

"And be subject to one another in the fear of Christ."
—Ephesians 5:21 (NASB)

The Bible tells us to be subject to one another. Other translations use the "S" word. You know, "submit" to one another. Yuck! No one likes the word, much less the idea of submitting to a spouse. This idea of submission is one of the most prevalent causes of our altercations, especially among Christians. After all, doesn't the Bible tell wives to "submit to your husband as unto the Lord."? Sure, and most wives would say they'd be glad to submit to their husbands when he treats them like the Lord does. For many, the hurts are so deep that we've already made an unconscious decision, "I will never submit to you!"

But nevertheless, we're called to submit, or be subject to one another. It's a mutual thing, and it begins with the husband, as the leader, submitting to his wife, honoring and esteeming her more highly than himself. Then she naturally responds by returning the honor. She submits to him, and now we are submitting to one another. Why? Out of reverence for, or in the fear of, Christ. In this context the word "fear" refers to an "extreme reverence, or awe, as toward a supreme power" (College Dictionary). So we are to submit to one another as an expression of our reverence for Christ. If we're not submitted to Christ first, there's no chance of being submitted to one another.

Too many of us, in our western style Christianity, have lost the sense of "the fear of the Lord." We've forgotten how to truly revere Christ, to honor Him, and yes, even submit to Him, and

His will for our lives. So naturally, we carry that same rebellion into our human relationships. We all struggle with the "S" word. Yet we need to be honest and open with God and confess our rebellion, self-righteousness and stubbornness, and submit ourselves to Jesus first, then to our spouses, in the fear, extreme reverence, and holy awe of our God.

Question for both of us: Do we really live in "the fear of the Lord?" How does it show? What practical steps can we take to reflect a greater sense of honor, reverence, and fear of Christ? What practical steps can we take to show honor and reverence for one another?

Prayer for both of us: Lord, we confess our rebellion and self-righteousness. Help us to truly live a life "in the fear of Christ" with a holy awe and reverence that will be reflected in the way we treat and love one another.

Journal . . .

Week #38

THE IN-HOUSE COUNSELOR

*"Though one can be overpowered, two can defend them-
selves. A cord of three strands is not quickly broken."*
—Ecclesiastes 4:12

We have had clients who, on occasion, would say to us, "We wish we could take you home with us to be there when we have our knock-down drag-out fights." Apparently, they feel that if a counselor were available in the heat of battle they would find resolution to some of their communication problems. The truth is that God has provided exactly that for each and every married couple. You have a live-in Counselor who is better than any human counselor. He is the ever-present Holy Spirit. The problem is that He isn't visible to the natural eye. He doesn't demand your attention. He is simply residing inside each believer waiting to be called upon to bring justice and grace into every situation. But just as the husband and the wife must agree to come to our office to listen to what we have to say, a husband and a wife must also agree to come to the place of acknowledging God's presence (the Holy Spirit) among them and listening to what He has to say. How do they do that? By praying and searching the Scriptures together; by setting aside their self interests and submitting themselves to the interests and will of God concerning their situation as revealed through the Word and prayer. The Holy Spirit will reveal the will of God that always tends toward reconciliation to Himself, then to one another. Paul tells us exactly where to find this Counselor: "Don't you know that you are God's temple and The Holy Spirit lives in you?" (1 Cor. 3:16).

The Holy Spirit is your in-house Counselor, but it will take both the husband and the wife to agree to an appointment to hear what He has to say. Go ahead. Set a time for both to seek His counsel concerning some of your issues. Listen to what He has to say, and trust Him. Human counselors make mistakes. This One doesn't. On that you can rest assured. The best part is that the fee for an unlimited number of sessions was already paid on a hill called Calvary, and He always has an opening for you. What a deal!

Question for both of us: When was the last time we both submitted ourselves to seeking counsel from the Holy Spirit together?

Prayer for both of us: Lord, help us to mutually submit to the counsel of Your Holy Spirit. Help us to call upon Him, daily, together, that this marriage will become all it can be, "a _cord of three strands is not quickly broken._"

Journal . . .

Week #39

THE LANGUAGE OF INTIMACY

"Many will say to me on that day, 'Lord, Lord, did we not prophesy in your name, and in your name drive out demons and perform many miracles?' Then I will tell them plainly, 'I never knew you. Away from me, you evildoers!' "—Matthew 7:22, 23

How could Jesus be so cruel to call His followers evildoers? After all, they were doing the work of the ministry. You know, prophesying, driving out demons and even working miracles! Yet Jesus rejected them. He said it was because He never knew them. The answer lies in the word He used when He said, "I never *knew* you." The word He used, in the original language, means "intimacy." What He was saying to these disciples was, "You and I were never intimate. There's no oneness. You are out there doing your own thing in My name, without abiding in Me; without taking the time to know Me, and let Me know you." You see, without intimacy you have ritual instead of relationship. What Jesus desires is relationship. What keeps marriages strong and healthy is not ritual but a relationship that grows out of deep intimacy.

How do we build intimacy? We build intimacy by sharing our feelings and needs with one another. You see, not all communicating builds relationship. There are five levels of communication from the most superficial to the most intimate. They are speaking in clichés, sharing facts, sharing opinions, sharing feelings and sharing needs. I can talk all day long to the guy on the corner in clichés, facts and opinions without building relationship. It's only when we get to share feelings and needs that we begin to build intimacy; that we really get to know one another. Without that all we have is ritual. The marriage may look good on the outside, but the reality is that we have no intimacy, no oneness. We really don't know each other. We need to learn how to be intimate with one another—and that doesn't mean having sex! We must first learn to be intimate with Christ. Open your heart to Him. Share your feelings and needs. He won't hurt you. Get to truly know Him. Then, and only then, will you be empowered to know and love your spouse with a godly love, for "He that knows (has an intimate relationship with) God knows love. He that knows not God knows not love for God is love" (1 John 4:8).

Question for both of us: How well do we do with our communication? Do we get past sharing clichés, facts and opinions? Do we feel we can safely share our true feelings and needs without fear of being judged, rejected, corrected or discounted?

Prayer for both of us: Lord, help us first know You. Then help us to know each other by taking the time to share our feelings and our needs. Help us to be bold and courageous. Help us find true intimacy with You, and with one another.

Journal . . .

Week #40

THE LIGHT IN YOU

"The eye is the lamp of the body. If your eyes are good your whole body will be full of light. But if your eyes are bad your whole body will be full of darkness. If then, the light that is within you is darkness, how great is that darkness!"
—Matthew 6:22-24

Each of us has a light source. If it is truly light then that light energy will be projected through our eyes, the lamps of our bodies. Everything we see will be lighted up. The grass will be greener. They sky will be bluer, because the light that is in you is projected on everything around you. But if that light in you is darkness then that darkness will be projected on everything. It will be like a shadow cast upon everything you look at. The grass will be drab and the sky will be gray. If the light in you is light you will see the things that God has given you in your relationship with your spouse. You will be counting your blessings. If the light in you is darkness, that darkness will be projected onto all the things God hasn't given you in your marriage. You will see the negatives, and not the positives. The lesson for marriage in these verses is that, though there are positives and negatives in every marriage, whether we're walking in the light of His love and joy, or in darkness and misery has more to do with the light source in us than the actual circumstances we're in. In His light we see light. If things look bleak out there it's time to check the light source in here!

Question for both of us: How have we seen our marriage, through the light that is in us, or has that light been more darkness? How?

88

Prayer for both of us: Lord, re-energize that light source in us that we may see our marriage in the light of Your love. Help us to magnify the positives and minimize the negatives. Help us to see the positives in each other, continually.

Journal . . .

Week #41

THE PLACE OF PEACE

"You will keep in perfect peace all who trust in you, whose thoughts are fixed on you."—Isaiah 26:3

Throughout our day-to-day lives, we often run into circumstances that one of us wants to change, but the other one is just not as willing, at least, not right now. In our humanity we want things to work as we plan, or at the very least, meet our minimum expectations for the situation. When was the last time you had your mind set on buying something, and your spouse just wasn't ready at the particular moment you were? Do you find yourself frustrated and tired of waiting on your mate? Some of us are of the mindset "I want it done yesterday," or "I want to do this now, my way."

Have you ever tried to invite God into such a situation? Can you see yourself asking Him to take control instead of yourself?

The next time you find yourself thinking like this, pull on the reigns of your mind. Tell yourself, out loud if you must, "WHOA!" Then command your mind to turn your thoughts and imaginations over to the Lord. Release all your expectations of the situation to the Lord, and just thank Him for the outcome.

When I am able to do this, immediate peace comes upon me, and I've even had my spouse set aside his agenda, and put me above his plans. When that happens it's really special because I know it's coming from his heart, not because he's just trying to keep me quiet. But it does take trust. It takes keeping my mind fixed on Him.

90

Question for both of us: Can we trust God for all these day-to-day situations, or do we feel we need to be in control, even in the little simple things? What does it look like in our relationship when we can trust Him? When we can't?

Prayer for both of us: Dear Lord, please help us to mutually agree to seek You in ALL things, and help us to love each other in spite of unmet expectations. Lord, help us to realize if You are first we can trust You for wisdom in all things. Keep us in Your perfect peace as our minds stay fixed on You.

Journal . . .

Week #42

THE POWER OF LIFE AND DEATH

" *The tongue has the power of life and death, and those who love it will eat its fruit.*"—Proverbs 18:21

I always thought it interesting that in the Genesis account of creation we're told that God created the earth, not by fashioning a lump of clay, or mixing up some earthly concoction in his chemistry lab, but rather we're told that "God said . . ." and "there was . . ." What a powerful word! He simply said it and it was! Jesus told His disciples that if they would "say" to this mountain be thou removed it would jump into the sea! Talk about power! I'd love to say, "bills be paid!" and see it happen. Oh well, I guess I'm still missing something.

But nevertheless, there is power in the spoken word to create or to destroy. I've seen too many people come into my counseling office living a life of defeat, never finding their potential, because of a parent who spoke defeat into their lives. The power of words! The tongue has the power of life and death. It is an instrument for creation or destruction. If you could visually see the words go out of your own mouth would you see them lifting up others or would it go toward putting them down? Would they build up or tear down? It's no wonder the Bible tells us we'll have to give account for every idle word that proceeds from our mouths. With our tongues we can create or destroy, bless or curse. Out of our mouths should pass nothing but truth, life and blessing. Let's create not destroy.

Question for both of us: What do I see coming out of your mouth, words that build up or words that tear down? What do you see coming out of my mouth?

Prayer for both of us: Lord, help us to let nothing pass through our lips that will destroy what You are trying to create in our lives. Help us to speak nothing but truth, life and blessing. Help us to be part of Your plan for creation.

Journal . . .

TRUTH AND GRACE

The Word became flesh and made his dwelling among us. We have seen his glory, the glory of the One and Only, who came from the Father, full of grace and truth. . . . From the fullness of his grace we have all received one blessing after another. For the law was given through Moses; grace and truth came through Jesus Christ."—John 1:14-17

Grace is the medium for truth. In an atmosphere of grace the truth can flow unhindered. In truth there is freedom to love, to learn and to grow. Truth and grace are partners that keep us balanced, and centered on Christ. Grace is the atmosphere in which truth can flow. It's not uncommon for a husband to hide a decision he has made from his wife, because he was afraid of what her reaction might be. It's not uncommon for Mom to keep things about the children from Dad, because she might be afraid he would be too hard on the children. No grace. In both cases there is no intent to lie to one another, the effect, in fact, is a lie. We are not walking in truth. In many cases husbands and wives are living lies, because there is no grace, and therefore no truth. A husband who is always angry, or a wife who is always nagging, make it impossible for truth to flow in an atmosphere of grace.

Jesus told us that we shall know the truth, and the truth will set us free. Before we can be freed by the truth we must establish the atmosphere in which truth can flow freely—the atmosphere of grace. God has shown us grace by not holding our many sins against us. Now it's up to us to extend that grace to others. If we have not received it personally, we don't have it to give. You'll only get frustrated. First you must choose to live for Christ, and receive His grace. Then you will have it to give to your spouse. Then truth can flow. Then you can grow together in His love in truth and grace.

Question for both of us: What is the atmosphere in our home? Is it grace, or is it strife and tension? Have I personally received the gift of God's grace by choosing to follow Christ? Then how can I extend that grace to my spouse in our day-to-day, hour-by-hour, moment-by-moment interactions?

Prayer for both of us: Lord, help us to receive the fullness of Your grace that we would have it for one another. Help us to establish an atmosphere of grace in our home so that truth will flow unhindered, so that our children may see what godly love is all about, and we will all grow in Your love, in Your Spirit, in Your truth and in Your grace.

Journal . . .

MARRIAGE AND POLITICS

"Then he said to them, 'Give to Caesar what is Caesar's, and to God what is God's.' "—Matthew 22:21

At first, one might wonder what in the world politics would have to do with marriage? The truth is politics has everything to do with marriage. First of all, marriage is an institution ordained by God, as a sacred union between a man and a woman. One of its primary purposes is to represent the eternal relationship God desires to have with His creation. We are betrothed to Him when we receive Christ as Savior. He, the Bridegroom, will come for His bride to consummate the marriage at the last trumpet call. Therefore, marriage is a sacred institution created by, defined by, and overseen by God Himself. This sacred institution is the very foundation for civil order. We, who are married, have the honor and privilege of representing this nature of God in the earth. Marriage is not about us. It's about God, His kingdom, and His order for a civil society.

Now it is the duty of civil authorities to help facilitate this divinely given institution without usurping God's authority by redefining it according to human whims. This institution, and in fact our civilization, is in dire peril as ungodly forces are intent on redefining marriage to mean the union of any two consenting adults regardless of gender. So-called "civil unions" serve to devalue the holy institution of marriage. Liberal politicians believe it is government who defines what marriage will be. They believe if two males, or two females want to be married the government should give them that legal right. They have no regard for God's divine authority.

They are their own ultimate authority. If liberal politicians gain political leadership, the sacred institution of marriage will be further devalued. There will be more societal chaos, and our children will grow up in a nation much different than the one that was handed to us.

We must fulfill our responsibility to our nation as part of our responsibility to God, to vote for godly men and women who will submit themselves to the divine authority of God. Jesus instructed us to give unto God what is God's, and unto Caesar what is Caesar's, namely, our informed vote. Whether our children grow up in a free nation "under God," or in a Socialistic state where politicians see themselves as gods will be determined, in large part, by the choice we make on Election Day. Marriage and the rest of societal order hang in the balance. The charge to us: ***Pray and Vote!***

Question for both of us: Who are we voting for, and why?

Prayer for both of us: Lord, help us to be the salt of the earth and the light of the world in our sphere of influence, by casting our informed vote and encouraging others to do the same. Help us to fight for marriage, and Your divine order for our nation so that our children may grow up in peace and godliness.

Journal . . .

Week #45

TWO ARE BETTER

"Two are better than one because they have a good return for their work: If one falls down his friend can help him up. But pity the man who falls and has no one to help him up. Also if two lie down together they will keep warm. But how can one keep warm alone? Though one may be overpowered two can defend themselves. A cord of three strands is not easily broken.—Ecclesiastes 4:9-12

The preacher here teaches about the benefits of working together, walking together, even sleeping together. Unless one has the gift of celibacy they are not really complete until there is unity with a spouse. Scripture tells us that the effectiveness of two is not just doubled, but it's multiplied. Deuteronomy 32:30 tells us that though one can put a thousand to flight two can put ten thousand to flight! No wonder the enemy of our souls has been so intent on destroying marriages. A solid married couple is the biggest threat to Satan's plans to destroy our families and culture. Many of the ills we see in our society today can be traced back to broken families. As the marriage goes, so goes the family, so goes the church, so goes the society. But a couple wrapped around Jesus—the picture of the cord of three strands—that is not easily broken. Nothing will be impossible for a husband and wife dedicated to keeping Christ in the center of their relationship, and wrapped tight around Him and one another. When we sense the spirit of strife approaching, that's when we have to close ranks against Satan. Let's forget about what we want and ask, "What is it that Jesus wants?" Two is a gift from God. A threefold cord is unbeatable!

Question for both of us: How have we been there for one another in times of need? How have we kept Christ in the center of our relationship, or how have we not?

Prayer for both of us: Lord, help us to appreciate the gift You've given us in marriage, and help us keep You in the center of our day to day lives. Be the Mediator in our relationship. Be the center strand. Help us stay wrapped around You tightly.

Journal . . .

Week #46

WHAT MATTERS MOST

"Just as man is destined to die once, and after that to face judgment."—Hebrews 9:27

This has been one of those weeks that you forget about the petty distractions of life and think about the things that really matter the most. Penny's mom passed into glory after struggling with illness. We were singing Amazing Grace around her bedside as she slipped into Jesus' arms. At the wake we really were impressed with the value of a shared faith and conviction in Christ. We know we'll see Mom again, because she knows Jesus. The Apostle John said, "I write these things that you may *know* that you have eternal life." (1 John 5:14). Penny and I were able to look at each other with a comforting expression of assurance that we know Mom is with Jesus, where we too, will be one day. Unfortunately, not everyone who came to pay their respects had that assurance. Many were brought up in church. Most believed in God. But many did not have that personal relationship with Jesus that can only come from a surrendered life, a life that places Christ on the throne, a life that seeks to bless Him instead of asking Him to bless us, a life that acknowledges God is my pilot, not my co-pilot. Whether one calls it "saved," "born again," "converted," whatever, the label isn't important. It's the conviction of heart that He is number one in my life. When that conviction is shared by husband and wife, there's a sense of oneness that provides the foundation of love and joy that allows us to go through even the difficult times of life with an inner conviction that God truly is working all things together for our good because we love Him. When this faith is shared by husband and wife, and there is a death in the family, it's just a reminder

100

that God is in the process of reconciling us to Him, and, in Him, we will be together forever in that place of eternal righteousness peace and joy. That's what matters most. ". . . *Man is destined to die once, and after that to face judgment*" (Hebrews 9:27).

Question for both of us: How much do we really share a common personal faith in Christ? Should our time on earth be cut short, are we ready to face Jesus?

Prayer for both of us: Lord, help us to share a common faith in Your Son, Jesus. Let Jesus be the Center around which our lives will revolve. Let Christ be that solid Foundation for our marriage, our family, for all that we say, think or do. Let us never lose sight of what matters most.

Journal . . .

Week #47

WHEN WE'RE APART

"I belong to my lover, and his desire is for me."
—Song of Solomon 7:10

In this day and age things are so busy; our commitments to our families and jobs leave us little time to just enjoy one another. Especially starving for time is the most important of human relationships—husband and wife.

The two of us become not only strangers in the night, as the song goes, but also throughout the day. What do you think about your time apart? I know some of us would say, "I can't wait for time alone." God does allow those times, but what do we really learn during our times apart?

Bill and I have spent one of our very few weekends apart this weekend, and at first I saw it as an opportunity to get things done that I wanted to do. I knew I would miss him, but I also knew I could accomplish so much with him away. I could actually have a time alone! Funny, instead of hearing God say, Come away with me," I sensed Him saying, "Can you really feel the absence of your other half? Do you see how much more you can become one? Do you see why you went through those difficult years in your marriage? Do you see why I am allowing this weekend?" Not what I expected, Lord!

As I lay my head down on the pillow 2:30 a.m Sunday morning my best friend wasn't with me. His caring arms weren't around me. Did I miss him? YOU BET I DID! Yet God was there and spoke of His love for me. So I rested! I awoke this morning knowing that God has done a great thing in my very own heart. I know that God has given me a special blessing in the spouse He provided—and even more than that—I know "I belong to my beloved and his desire is for me." I am awaiting Bill's return with an excited anticipation of renewing our love affair all over again. I want to, once again, receive the gift God has so graciously given to me.

Question for both of us: How do I feel when we're apart? Have we learned to appreciate each other sufficiently so that when we are apart we feel a sense of loss?

Prayer for both of us: Lord, help us to take time daily to connect so that we can build an intimacy that will result in a sense of loss and appreciation for one another when we are apart.

Journal . . .

WHO OR WHAT?

"The LORD God said, 'It is not good for the man to be alone. I will make a helper suitable for him.' "—Genesis 2:18

Imagine waking up one morning, stepping out your door and seeing the arm of God stretching down through the clouds to hand you a gift wrapped in beautiful paper with a note on it, which said, "Do Not Open Until Christmas." What would you do with such a gift? Why? You don't even know what's in the box! Would you take it home and care for it? Would you value it? Would you handle it with care? Why should you? For all you know it could be a lump of coal in the box. "But that's not important," you say; what's important is the fact that this gift was given to you, personally, by God Himself. Whatever is in the box is special, because of the One who gave it to you. That's why you'll value it, and guard it with your life. Now what will happen when Christmas comes and you open it to find a piece of coal? Would you discard it, or continue to value it because of who gave it to you? If you look at it simply for what it is there would be no reason to care for it, but if you'll see it for who gave it to you, it will be your most prized possession.

So it is in marriage. If we look at each other for what we are, we all fall short. We never measure up. If you love one another for what they are, chances are, there won't be too much reason to love. We see the faults in one another. It's like we brought home that beautifully wrapped gift from the church when we said, "I do." Then when we got home we started unwrapping it to discover a hunk of coal. Now what do we do with it? Do we build disdain for it because it isn't what we thought it was, or will we value it for who gave it to us— God Himself?

What my spouse is will always fall short of my standard, just as I will fall short of hers. I can't love her for what she is. Thank God, He didn't love me for what I am. I'm a self-centered sinner. But He loved me for who I am: His very own creation. I need to love my spouse for who she is: God's gift to me to complete me where I am incomplete, a helper suitable for me. She was given to me by the very hand of God. Wow!

Even though I may see a hunk of coal, the truth is more accurately what I fail to see—a diamond in the making! So let us love one another not for what we are but for who we are—God's gift to complete us where we are incomplete.

Question for both of us: Do I love you for who you are—God's gift to me to complete me, or do I see you for what you are, with all your shortcomings and faults?

Prayer for both of us: Lord, help us to see the hand that gave us to one another. Help us not to see just a hunk of coal, but to appreciate that we are Your gift to one another to help complete and balance our character. Help us to realize that we're both just a couple of hunks of coal, but in Your hands we're diamonds in the making. Help us to love each other, not for what we are but for who we are.

Journal . . .

Week #49

BREAK THE CURSE (Preparing for Christmas)

"You shall not make for yourself an idol in the form of anything in heaven above or on the earth beneath or in the waters below. You shall not bow down to them or worship them; for I, the LORD your God, am a jealous God, punishing the children for the sin of the fathers to the third and fourth generation of those who hate me, but showing love to a thousand generations of those who love me and keep my commandments."—Deuteronomy 20:4-6

As we begin preparations for the Christmas season we will probably be asking, "What is the best gift I can give for my children?" It's easy to get caught up in the commercialism of the day and simply let the advertisers make that decision for us. Sure, we'll listen to the child to hear what they want. Then we'll listen to the advertisers to hear what they say. Then we'll look for a match and go for it, and think we're doing a pretty good job. But ask the question, "How have these kinds of gifts really benefited my child in the past?" The sad stories of children lost to the gods of this world are endless. Whether we want to hear it or not, the truth is that our children are living under the curse of fathers who have not followed Christ. This curse will be on them, "to the third and fourth generation," and as each generation continues to turn their hearts against Christ, they extend the curse for yet another three or four generations. So the curse is perpetuated, until someone puts a stop to it by choosing to turn their hearts toward God. God's response is that he will show love to a thousand generations to those who would love Him. The challenge to us is to choose whether we will we go on buying gifts that have no relevance to the well-being of our children, or choose to give

106

a gift that will deliver them from the curse. What is that gift? —Parents who love God, and demonstrate it by their lifestyle. As the commercial says, there are some things you can't buy with Visa (or MasterCard, whichever it is). What will we pass on to our children this Christmas season: more meaningless toys, or the love of God? The choice, as always, is in our hands, and in our hearts.

Question for both of us: What are we passing on to our children this Christmas? Are we perpetuating the curse, or demonstrating the love of God in our home and in our relationships?

Prayer for both of us: Lord, help us to take Your commandments seriously. Help us to realize that our children do live under a curse because we have not loved You. Help us to turn our hearts away from our selfish motives and devices. Help us turn toward You, and demonstrate that love to our children, that they might be rescued from the power of the curse.

Journal . . .

Week #50

<u>WHO TO PLEASE</u>

"Am I now trying to win the approval of men, or of God? Or am I trying to please men? If I were still trying to please men, I would not be a servant of Christ."—Galatians 1:10

I remember an old Bob Dylan song in which he said, "Everybody's gotta please somebody." Well, I can tell you this much; if you're trying to please your husband or your wife, give it up. It just won't happen. "What kind of marriage counseling is this?" you say. It's the kind that is based in truth. We are so fickle as human beings that what pleases us today will probably not please us tomorrow. It's like trying to hit a moving target. It's a losing proposition. Let's be real. Has it worked for you? There's a better way, one that works. Live your life, not to please your spouse, or anyone else. Live your life to please God. First of all, God doesn't change. What pleases Him today will please Him tomorrow. It's a goal much more attainable. Secondly, if you're loving your spouse in a way that's pleasing to God, chances are your spouse will be pleased. It will be, in fact, the love of God expressed through you. Wow! It will be a love directed by your spouse's needs, though not necessarily their wants. It will be a love rooted in the wisdom of God, and energized by the power of His Spirit working in you. It will be a love that transcends human fickleness. It's a matter of changing focus. Get your sights off of trying to please each other, and fix them on pleasing God with the way you love each other. Everyone will be pleased, and God will get the glory! After all, "Everybody's gotta please somebody." It may as well be the one who can be pleased!

Question for dialogue: In what ways have we tried to please each other that just never seemed to work? How can we better please God with the way we love each other?

Prayer for both of us: "Lord, help us to live for one single purpose: To please You with the way we love and treat each other, so that Your love will freely flow through our lives and our home."

Journal . . .

WHY HAVEN'T I DIED YET, LORD?

"I have been crucified with Christ. It is no longer I that live, but Christ lives in me, and the life which I now live in the flesh, I live by faith in the Son of God who loved me and gave himself for me."—Galatians 2:20

Have you ever had one of those days when you just want to jump out of your life, and into some imaginary land where there is nothing but immediate gratification and happy endings? But then you find yourself coming back to reality, a reality in which you are often displeased with yourself. You find yourself saying and doing things you know you're not proud of. And wherever you go, there you are! Have you thought, "I'm a believer; I can't believe I said that. These words, and actions are not me!" Guess what? We all have those days. They seem to sneak up on us when we're not looking. When we blow it, it's time to go to the Lord and ask for forgiveness from God, then from each other. It's time to extend grace as we both strain forward. Take time afterward to examine what happened. While you're talking about it make a point of being tenderhearted toward one another. Remember, you both blow it from time to time. Ask God to tenderize your heart. (Ephesians 4:32)

You say, "He said mean and nasty things to me," "She said hurtful things that made me feel like less than a man." So what! How can we work through these nasty words that seem to slice us to pieces, and make us feel like a little child, sitting in a corner, shivering and afraid to come out? There is only one way that we can triumph over these real feelings to reconnect with our spouse in a loving, harmonious relationship. I didn't say it was easy. It isn't easy, but it is worth it, because

110

it's not about us. It's about the Kingdom. Die! Die to self. Haven't we claimed to be crucified with Christ? It is not we who live, but Christ in us? This is where the rubber meets the road, or more precisely, where our flesh meets the Cross. You know, where your will and His will "cross." Let His light shine on the darkness that it may be peeled away and die. Only then will we be in a position to know reconciliation first with Christ, then with each other.

Question for both of us: When was the last time we blew it? Were we able to give grace to one another? Why or why not? How can we handle such a situation better next time?

Prayer for both of us: Dear Heavenly Father, please forgive us for not fighting the good fight—the fight to overcome the flesh. Forgive us for hurting each other. Help us to have grace for one another even as You continually have grace for us. Help us learn from our mistakes. Help us to die to ourselves that we might live for Christ and for one another.

Journal . . .

YOU HAVE AN ENEMY

"It is to a man's honor to avoid strife, but every fool is quick to quarrel."—Proverbs 20:3

Are we honorable, or are we fools? Do we avoid strife, or are we quick to quarrel? Few principles will enrich your marriage more than the principle of avoiding strife. One of the most important things we've learned, one thing that has done more to change our relationship perhaps more than any other, is coming to realize that we are not each other's enemy, *but we do have an enemy—the spirit of strife!*

The spirit of strife is on assignment to destroy your marriage. To allow him to be lord in your home is to allow certain disaster. When he is detected husband and wife must close ranks, regardless of internal squabbles to defend against this outside enemy who is sure to cause disorder, anger and resentment. He desires to cause feelings of hatred between spouses when, in fact, that hatred should be directed at him. We must avoid strife at all costs if the marriage is to succeed. It won't matter who's right about an issue if there is no marriage. If someone has to win the argument, let it be your spouse. You'll be amazed at how the world won't come to an end! Furthermore, the spirit of strife will be defeated. If you can't let the other win the argument, take a time out by mutual agreement. Come back to the issue later when the air isn't so emotionally charged by the spirit of strife. Do whatever it takes. Just don't let strife take control. Ephesians 6:12 tells us, "For our struggle is not against flesh and blood (each other) but against the rulers, against the authorities, against the powers of this dark world, and against the spiritual forces of evil (the spirit of strife), in the heavenly realms (the atmosphere between the two of you).

The ultimate question is "Who will be lord in your life, the spirit of strife or the Prince of Peace?"

Question for both of us: When does the spirit of strife generally try to attack our marriage? What are some ways we can agree on, in advance, to avoid the spirit of strife from taking over?

Prayer for both of us: "Lord, You said that whatever we bind on earth will be bound in heaven, and whatever we loose on earth will be loosed in heaven. We, therefore, bind the spirit of strife from having further effect in our marriage, and we loose the spirit of grace and peace. Help us Father to allow Your Holy Spirit to take control, so that the spirit of strife won't be.

Journal . . .

Special Days

VALENTINE'S DAY AND MARRIAGE

"My lover spoke and said to me, 'Arise, my darling, my beautiful one, and come with me. See! The winter is past; the rains are over and gone. Flowers appear on the earth; the season of singing has come, the cooing of doves is heard in our land. The fig tree forms its early fruit; the blossoming vines spread their fragrance. Arise, come, my darling; my beautiful one, come with me.' "—Song of Songs 2:10-13

When did Valentine's Day begin? One legend contends that Valentine was a priest who served during the third century in Rome. When Emperor Claudius II decided that single men made better soldiers than those with wives and families, he outlawed marriage for young, single men—his crop of potential soldiers. Valentine, realizing the injustice of the decree, defied Claudius and continued to perform marriages for young lovers in secret. When Valentine's actions were discovered, Claudius ordered that he be put to death. Other stories suggest that Valentine may have been killed for attempting to help Christians escape harsh Roman prisons where they were often beaten and tortured.

There are still those today who would devalue the sacred institution of marriage. Turn on the T.V. any day of the week and you'll see romance and sex with everyone but a married couple. No wonder our divorce rate is so high in this country! It's time to recapture the romance, the excitement, the ecstasy (the real thing) that comes from enjoying the most sacred institution God has given to human creation. After all, it was given to be a model of our relationship with Him. As our marriage goes, so goes our relationship with our Maker. The opposite is true as well. As we renew our relationship with God, our marriage is also renewed. It can be no other way.

Love is a God thing. "Mutual use" is man's godless substitute. It doesn't work. So today, as Valentine did, let's fight for our marriages, even if we be put to death; let's celebrate, enjoy and defend the greatest institution this world has ever know.

Question for both of us: Do we really value and celebrate our gift of marriage? What special gift can I give my spouse this Valentine's Day that will communicate how much I really appreciate and value our God ordained relationship?

Prayer for both of us: Lord, help us to value dearly this greatest gift You have given us. Help us to renew our romance, to celebrate our love that You would receive the glory.

Journal . . .

MARRIAGE AND RESURRECTION

"But if it is preached that Christ has been raised from the dead, how can some of you say that there is no resurrection of the dead? If there is no resurrection of the dead, then not even Christ has been raised. And if Christ has not been raised, our preaching is useless and so is your faith."

—1 Corinthians 15:12-14

What does resurrection have to do with marriage? The resurrection proved that the Bible is true, and Jesus is credible. His methods work. He wasn't just a prophet. He is God! The resurrection validated everything he said. He said, "I am the Way" There is no other. He said if you try to keep your life you will lose it, but if you give up your life for His sake you will surely find it. He said unless a kernel of wheat falls to the ground and dies it can produce nothing but if it will fall to the ground, and die, it will produce a harvest. He lived and demonstrated the truth of what He taught by willingly giving up His own life for you and me on the cross. Then, true to His word, God raised Him up from the dead and gave Him the ultimate victory. Because of that demonstrated truth we can trust Him to give us victory if, we too, will humble ourselves, take upon ourselves the blame for all the failure in the marriage, warranted or not, and simply give up our lives, our pride, our rights, for the sake of my spouse and the marriage. The truth of the resurrection gives us the faith to believe that if we would refuse to defend ourselves, as Jesus refused to defend himself in the face of His accusers, God will raise us up as He did His own Son. Faith in the resurrection gives us faith in God's power to save our marriage if we would humble ourselves to the point of dying to all our ego, pride, and even our own sense of justice. God is faithful. Today we are living on the resurrection side of life, which never would have been possible without a crucifixion of our own self-life. The resurrection gives us the faith to do "whatever it takes" knowing that God's ways are true. It works!

Question for both of us: What does the resurrection mean to us personally? Do we really trust Christ with our whole lives?

Prayer for both of us: Lord, help us to understand the power of the resurrection so that we will be able to lay our lives down for one another, regardless of the circumstances, and give You the opportunity to manifest resurrection power in our own lives and marriage.

Journal . . .

MOTHER'S DAY—WHEN SHE'S GONE

"Out of all the peoples on the face of the earth, the Lord has chosen you to be His treasured possession."
—Deuteronomy 14:2

The month of May is quickly passing by, as are so many important events in our lives. Today is Mother's Day. All across the nation women are being honored. So, Happy Mother's Day to all the moms out there! May God bless you abundantly!

But how do we celebrate if we have lost a mom like I have recently? You see, she went home to be with the Lord as we were singing "Amazing Grace" at her hospital bedside. What do we do when we lose a mother, wife, sister, daughter or any woman who has filled this role in our lives? Do we try to ignore the day? Do we close ourselves off from all others? Do we weep and mourn for the woman who meant so much to us?

We can try to go on with life as though nothing happened. We can even be angry with God, or we can choose to remember how God has blessed us with our moms, and how He continues to love us through every circumstance. Remember, He chose us. We are His treasure.

What if we just ask Him, "How do You want me to celebrate this Mother's Day, Lord?" Perhaps God desires that we seek Him for the comfort we need when we lose such a treasure as our moms. As we yield our hearts to the Maker of us all, He will show us how to respond, in love, to celebrate the lives of the women who have loved us, who have sacrificed, and who have cared for us the best way they knew how.

Question for both of us: Are we able to mutually agree how to bless our moms? Are we showing our gratitude for the mom we have, or the mom we lost, by the life we are living?

Prayer for both of us: Lord help us to see our moms, wives, sisters or daughters as Your blessings to us. Help us to honor them as Your chosen vessels. Help us to be grateful for the gift of motherhood.

Journal . . .

MEMORIAL DAY—WHY REMEMBER?

"This is my commandment that you love one another just as I have loved you. Greater love has no one than this, that one lay down his life for his friends."—Jesus , John 15:12, 13

Why should we honor those who have fallen in battle so many years ago? What does Memorial Day have to do with my marriage? Lots! Marriage is based on a commitment to love. We need to honor those who have fallen because they exemplify the essence of love rooted in commitment. They gave everything they had to give that you and I might know the freedom we enjoy. They gave all. We can learn from them. I spent four years in the Air Force during the Viet Nam War. We had been married only eight months when I had to leave to go overseas, not to return to my new bride for 13 months. God kept me safe in Korea, but I lost friends in Viet Nam. Honoring them helps to teach me what love is, not a feeling, not having someone in my life to meet all my needs or wants. Love is giving. It's giving of all that I have without any guarantee, or even expectation, of getting anything in return. At the time I enlisted there were many selfishly running off to Canada because they weren't prepared to give. They weren't prepared to love. Today, in the same way, many husbands and wives are running off to their own places of escape to avoid giving their reasonable service because it may cost something. We need to be men and women of courage. We need to be prepared to give no matter the cost. When we look at the flag let the red stripes remind us of the blood that flowed to win our freedom, not just on the battlefields of war, but also the blood that flowed down Calvary's hill to win our freedom from sin, hell, death and the grave. We are free to know love because of those who went before us, loving us, purchasing our freedom with their lives, including the Son of

122

God. We can do no less. Let us remember and commit to carrying on the tradition of loving, no matter the cost.

Question for both of us: Whom do we know that has given their lives for our freedom? Are we prepared to pledge all that we have for each other, though it may cost our very lives?

Prayer for both of us: Lord, help us to be courageous enough to serve without concern for our own safety or convenience. Inspire us, Lord, to follow the example of those who went before us. Help us to give, so that the next generation might know the freedom and love You have shown to us.

Journal . . .

HER PERSPECTIVE ON FATHER'S DAY

"But I want you to understand That Christ is the head of every man, and the man is the head of the woman, and God is the head of Christ."—1 Corinthians11:3

We just celebrated Father's Day. Although many homes today are without a natural father, we can be grateful that we all have a perfect Heavenly Father. We can be grateful that there is Someone who is in control, who is bigger than you or me. He is God, our Father.

As a wife, I often thank God that I am not the man in my family. The role of husband and father is a difficult one. As wives, we have a clear role in serving the Lord by being the helper, and complement our husbands' need, but it's up to them to figure out what God's will is for this family and lead the way.

Think about your husband. Do you sometimes feel resentful because he seems to think he only has to go to work, and that's where his responsibility ends? Do you often feel like you have to do everything else? I understand, but you know it really is tough out there, "on the job." They need our help, encouragement, support and prayers as much as we need theirs.

Have you paid much attention to your responses to your husband? Are they gentle, and kind? Do you respond to him with a loving spirit? Does your husband feel honored, or does he feel like just one of the kids, or even worse, someone that is just there for the paycheck?

Wives, have you spent time with the Lord interceding for God's gift to you: your companion, your lover and friend? Do you ask your husband, "How can I pray for you?" You see, it's really not about us, or them, or even our children. It is about God! It is a Kingdom issue. It is an issue of our hearts.

Question: Am I a woman of God in my home? In my heart? In my relationship with my husband? Am I interceding for my husband on a daily basis? Can we pray together in submission to God, and in mutual submission to one another?

Pray: Our Heavenly Father, we know that our marriage has its ups and downs. Help us to be submitted first to You, then to one another in mutual submission. Help us to press forward toward the prize for Your glory, and for the Kingdom!

Journal . . .

FATHER'S DAY

"For this reason I kneel before the Father, from whom his whole family in heaven and on earth derives its name."
—Ephesians 3:14

All of human creation derives its name from "Father." It is from our Father in heaven that we find the source of our very existence. As majestic, and awesome as our heavenly Father is, He has shared His title with us. With that title comes the responsibility of being the Father God has called us to be. As I look back on my own years of fathering, I'm first of all, so grateful for the adults my children have become. The truth is I believe they have become the adults they are more in spite of my fathering skills than because of them. I'm no different than most fathers my age who look back and realize we have put our time and energy in the wrong places while our children were growing up, and we can't go back to do it over. We've spent all our time focusing primarily on building a career and raising a family on the side, instead of focusing on raising a family first, then the career on the side. While Bill Jr. and Dulcinea were growing up I was so focused on the job that I missed so many opportunities to let the Father's love flow through me into their hearts. I had all the right reasons. I was planting a new church then. Of course, everybody else needed me. The truth is I was so busy saving the world that I was neglecting my own family. If I had it to do over again, I certainly would spend more quality time with each of my children building relationship, learning what interests and concerns each one of them have. I would have spent more time fathering them. What would have been the measure of my success? When each child truly felt they were most important to me after God and their mom. I'm thankful that God has seen fit to allow Bill Jr. and Dulce to stay living with us for a while, giving us the opportunity to make up for some of those years. That's not the case for so many families.

It's my most fervent prayer that the men who come into our counseling room will not repeat the mistakes of my generation. We must take fathering seriously. The minds and hearts of the next generation are being shaped through the love of their fathers. Let's get it right, for their well being, and our Father's glory.

Question for Dad: How well do I communicate to my children that they are the most important thing to me next to God and Mom? How do my actions confirm or contradict this statement?

Prayer for Dad: Lord, help me to be the father You've called me to be; to make the changes I must to get my priorities straight, to get my actions in line with my words so that the next generation will have a better sense of the Father's love than my generation. Help me to have no regrets concerning my role as Dad. Help me love my children as You love me.

Journal . . .

CHANGING SEASONS

"There is a time for everything, and a season for every activity under heaven: a time to be born and a time to die, a time to plant and a time to uproot, a time to kill and a time to heal, a time to tear down and a time to build, a time to weep and a time to laugh, a time to mourn and a time to dance, a time to scatter stones and a time to gather them, a time to embrace and a time to refrain, a time to search and a time to give up, a time to keep and a time to throw away, a time to tear and a time to mend, a time to be silent and a time to speak, a time to love and a time to hate, a time for war and a time for peace. What does the worker gain from his toil? I have seen the burden God has laid on men. He has made everything beautiful in its time. He has also set eternity in the hearts of men; yet they cannot fathom what God has done from beginning to end."—Ecclesiastes 3:1-11

The trees are shedding their leaves. The air is cool and crisp. Another season of change; Election Day is this week. There will even be a change in our national leadership. In these latter days it seems like changes are coming faster and more furious than ever. We must be as the sons of Issachar who understood the times and knew what to do. We must be able to manage the times given to us in the midst of so much change. I believe with all my heart that this is a time to heal, a time to build. We must endeavor to build relationships, especially with our spouses and families. In this fast and furious culture we've forgotten relationships. We're too busy working to provide for our families while sacrificing relationship with them. What kind of sense does that make? What does the worker gain from his toil? Is he but chasing after the wind? Let's stop running around like mindless gerbils running aimlessly in a cage that spins endlessly but goes nowhere. It's time to reorder our lives in the midst of a changing world. Let's stop to discern the times. What season is this in our own lives? How can we embrace positive change? What changes must we make in our priorities, in our schedules, in our vision and goals for our lives. (You do have a vision, don't you?) Write them down. Where do we want to be spiritually, in our marriage, in our family, in our careers, six months from now, a year from now, five years from now? This is a good time to meditate on where we are in life, and where we want to be. There will be change. That, you can't avoid. But whether those changes move us toward order and peace will be determined by whether we can exercise the mind God gave us to understand the times, and know what to do, remembering always to keep an eye on that eternity which God has already set in our hearts.

Question for both of us: What's changing in our lives? How are things different than they were last year at this time? What changes in priorities and schedules do we have to make?

Prayer for both of us: Lord, help us to make a sober assessment of the times we live in. Help us to assess our relationships, and to make it a priority to build relationship in our own homes first, then with others. Help us order our lives in such a way that we will be prepared to enter into eternity when You call. It could be today.

Journal . . .

THANKSGIVING
GRATEFUL OR GRUMBLER?

"Be joyful always; pray continually; give thanks in all circumstances, for this is God's will for you in Christ Jesus."
— 1 Thessalonians 5:16-18

One of the classic "oldies" we used to sing in my teen singing group days in Brooklyn, declared, "There are just two kinds of people in the world. They are a boy and girl." I realize now that there really are just two kinds of people in the world, though I'm not talking about boys and girls. I'm talking about the grateful and the grumblers. (And I confess, I still haven't been delivered from the spirit of "oldies.") We know God makes us boy or girl, but what makes us grateful or grumblers? You see, we all have things that God has given us and done for us, as well as things He hasn't given us or done for us. We all have this simple fact in common. But whether we walk in joy or misery depends on which of those two realities we allow to dwell in our minds. If I continually see and think of all that God has given me, and done in my life, I develop a heart of gratitude. Out of that heart springs up a fountain of joy! If, on the other hand, I dwell on all that God hasn't given me, or done for me, I develop a grumbling heart, which eventually turns into a bitter pool. You know a few of those people, don't you? You know, the ones whose stone cold face hasn't cracked a genuine smile in ages. You just know every word out of their mouths is going to be a complaint or criticism. What a sad life! In fact I can't think of anything more sad than an unbelieving grumbler. Imagine living a life of misery here, only to be followed by an eternity in hell! Bummer! The good news is that we can choose to live in joy by choosing to dwell on all that God has given us and done for us. We're not denying the negatives. We're honestly acknowledging them, but we're not allowing them to dwell in our minds. I'm living in the positives. That's where I dwell. That's my mental address. The more I dwell there, the more grateful I become, the more joy springs up from within me. That's the abundant life Jesus spoke of! There are just two kinds of people in the world—the grateful and the grumblers. I've chosen to be in the first group. (If you really want to know what God does with grumblers read Numbers Chapter 14. It isn't pretty.) We have a lot to be thankful for. Let's be counted among the grateful.

Question for both of us: Which group do we tend to fall in, the grateful or the grumblers? Why?

Prayer for both of us: Lord, help us keep our minds focused on all You have done for us and all You have given us. Help us to soberly acknowledge the negatives, but help us live in the positives that we may enter into each new day with thanksgiving in our hearts and praise on our lips to realize the abundant life You have promised us.

Journal . . .

Love Is . . .

LOVE IS PATIENT

"Love is patient, love is kind. It does not envy, it does not boast, it is not proud. It is not rude, it is not self-seeking, it is not easily angered, it keeps no record of wrongs. Love does not delight in evil but it rejoices with the truth. It always protects, always trusts, always hopes, always perseveres. Love never fails. . . ."—1 Corinthians 13:4-8

Sometimes the King James Version says it best. It translates patience as "long-suffering." And what does long-suffering mean? Suffering long! That's it! "But I've suffered long enough!" you say. Oh, have you? Look at the palms of your hands. See any nail scars there? Then you haven't suffered as much as Christ has suffered for you. Put another way; you haven't been as patient with others as Christ has been patient with you. He is patient with us, and continues to accept us and love us for who we are, not what we are. He continues to forgive us even while we're in the act of sin, provided of course that our hearts are really turned toward Him, and we desire to do His will. Husbands and wives are both struggling to change day by day. The key is to be patient with one another as we are both struggling. Let's be encouraging for whatever progress we see, and not become impatient because we're not seeing more. It will come. Don't push it. Enjoy the ride. Paul tells us we need two things to see all that God has reserved for us: faith and patience (Hebrews 6:12). When we blow it, it's usually because we don't have the faith or patience to persevere. We're just not willing to suffer long enough to see the breakthrough. Be patient with one another, forgiving one another, just as God, in Christ Jesus forgave you.

Love is patient. To the extent that we are patient we are loving. To the extent that we are not, we are not loving. That's truth!

134

Question for dialogue: "How have we been impatient with one another? How does it affect our relationship and the atmosphere in our home?

Prayer for both of us: "Lord, help us to be patient with one another, even when it means suffering long. When we need strength to go on, help us come to You, our Source, our Strength, until through faith and patience we see the fullness of all You've promised."

Journal . . .

LOVE IS KIND

Love is patient, <u>love is kind</u>. It does not envy, it does not boast, it is not proud. It is not rude, it is not self-seeking, it is not easily angered, it keeps no record of wrongs. Love does not delight in evil but it rejoices with the truth. It always protects, always trusts, always hopes, always perseveres. Love never fails. . . . "—1 Corinthians 13:4-8

What is kind? I mean, it's a nice sounding word, but where can we see it in real life, particularly in this fast paced society where everyone is busy expressing their anger and demanding their rights? After all, when was the last time you even heard the word "kind" on a T.V. sitcom lately, other than deciding what "kind" of pizza to send out for. But then, that's not the kind of kind we're talking about. Unfortunately, kindness is not exactly in vogue in our culture, but it's absolutely essential to a healthy loving relationship. So we need to swim against the modern currents to do what Paul tells us: ". . . be tenderhearted and kind." Kindness is being tenderhearted. It can best be seen and heard in our tone of voice. Is there softness in our speech? Is there a tender heart behind the way we address one another? Or is there gruffness, hardness? Do we sound annoyed, angry or frustrated? If that's the case, we need to learn to be tenderhearted and kind. We need to replace our gruffness with softness, our insensitivity with tenderness. One way to do this is to think about your spouse, "I love you," before you speak. Just bringing that truth to the forefront of your awareness will change your countenance and the very spirit behind your words. It's easy enough to be angry, frustrated or annoyed. That's natural. Let's choose to do what's unnatural: be tenderhearted and kind. To the extent that we are being kind we are loving. To the extent that we aren't being kind, we aren't loving. That's the plain and simple truth.

Question for dialogue: When do we find it most difficult to be tenderhearted and kind to one another? How can we work on reminding ourselves to be gentle, soft, tenderhearted and kind?

Prayer for both of us: Lord, help us to be tenderhearted and kind with one another. Remind us to think, "I love you." before we speak. Help us to model that tenderhearted and kind demeanor that will help our children grow into tenderhearted and kind adults.

Journal . . .

LOVE DOES NOT ENVY

"Love is patient, love is kind. It does not envy, it does not boast, it is not proud. It is not rude, it is not self-seeking, it is not easily angered, it keeps no record of wrongs. Love does not delight in evil but it rejoices with the truth. It always protects, always trusts, always hopes, always perseveres. Love never fails. . . ."—1 Corinthians 13:4-8

In just a few months I'll be turning fifty-one, and I believe it's only been in these last few years that I have come to really know how love does not envy. I remember my days as a younger preacher, how I would look at T.V. ministries with their large following, and think to myself, "Someday. . . ." I felt it was all right to put up with a small church, as long as it was going to get me a much larger ministry down the road. By envying others, and coveting what I didn't have, I truly missed out on the joy of knowing what I did have. That's the problem with envy. It distracts you from enjoying what you have by getting you to fantasize over what you don't have. Envy will not only steal your joy, but it will turn it into grumbling, and eventually, into anger. You will begin to believe that you actually deserve what you envy, and circumstances, or maybe other people, are keeping you from what you really deserve. You will come to resent others or your circumstances. You'll be miserable. Envy keeps us from knowing the joy of the now, the God of the now. Today, when our family sits around the table for dinner, and the conversation gets downright hilarious, I often become overwhelmed with joy, thinking of the love that we have in our home. We have no big T.V. ministry, no big church, no big home or fancy car, but what we have is love. What joy! There's no sense of envy. I already have more than what I deserve. Why miss the joy of the now? Life is too short. Thank God I don't have what I deserve, or I'd be burning in hell about now. As Paul said, "I have learned to be content in whatever state I'm in." It took me a while to learn that lesson. It's my prayer for you that you'll be just a little quicker to learn then I was.

Question for dialogue: What are some of the things we find ourselves coveting? Who do we envy, and why?

Prayer for both of us: Lord, help us to focus on the now; to be content in whatever state we're in. Help us to be grateful for whatever it is we have, instead of envying others. Help us to know that what we have is what You've determined is right and good for us for today. Help us to realize that if all we have is Jesus, we already have more than we deserve.

Journal . . .

LOVE DOES NOT BOAST

"Love is patient, love is kind. It does not envy, <u>it does not boast,</u> it is not proud. It is not rude, it is not self-seeking, it is not easily angered, it keeps no record of wrongs. Love does not delight in evil but it rejoices with the truth. It always protects, always trusts, always hopes, always perseveres. Love never fails. . . ."—1 Corinthians 13:4-8

Nothing turns me off more than someone blowing their own horn trying to convince the world that they are so great and wonderful. Most of us can recognize that behavior in social settings pretty easily, but in marriage, boasting takes a more subtle nature, but it's just as repulsive. Real love doesn't look to promote itself, because it's too busy looking to promote others. The two are mutually exclusive. *"Let no unwholesome word proceed out of your mouth, but only that which is good for building up of others according to their need"* (Eph. 4:29). You can't build up others while you're building up yourself. Leave that up to God. He can do a much better job than you can. He wants to build you up to others, but you have to let Him do it by getting out of the way. Get out of self-promotion, or even self-defending, and get into promoting your spouse, defending your spouse. Be the president of your spouse's fan club, the captain of their cheerleading team. Choose to walk in humility, a choice that says I will not defend myself, promote myself, or try to lift myself above any other. I will leave that up to God. Instead, I will give my life to promoting others, to building them up in any way I can. Nobody loves a braggart, or one who is promoting or defending themselves. Leave that up to God, and choose to be one who will give their lives to bragging on others, promoting others, defending others, the first of which will be your spouse, and believe me, God will take care of bragging on you.

Question for dialogue: When do I feel that you tend to brag or boast about yourself in ways that cause me to feel negatively toward you?

Prayer for both of us: Lord, help us to focus on lifting up each other instead of promoting, bragging, or even defending ourselves. Help us to be each other's number one cheerleader, and to trust You for our own promotion.

Journal . . .

LOVE IS NOT PROUD

"Love is patient, love is kind. It does not envy, it does not boast, it is not proud. It is not rude, it is not self-seeking, it is not easily angered, it keeps no record of wrongs. Love does not delight in evil but it rejoices with the truth. It always protects, always trusts, always hopes, always perseveres. Love never fails. . . ."—1 Corinthians 13:4-8

Love is not proud? What does that mean? Often we think of pridefulness, as someone "struttin' their stuff," or thinking of themselves as better than others in very visible ways. Here is a definition of pride that will change you forever if you'll take hold of it. Ready? Here it goes:

> *Pride isn't thinking too much of yourself.*
> *It's thinking of yourself too much!*

That's right. It's possible to be prideful even while you're putting yourself down, saying, "Woe is me. I'm just not worthy, just not good enough." Your focus is still on yourself! You're focused on yourself just as much as the person who thinks too highly of himself or herself. You're still thinking of yourself! You can't be thinking of the other person's well being. You're too self-focused. That's pride! Never mind you're unworthiness. God doesn't make junk. You're worthy because he makes you worthy. And guess what? You're no better than the next guy. You have nothing that God didn't give you, and nothing he can't take back in a moment. So you have nothing to focus on about yourself, either thinking too highly of yourself, or thinking too lowly of yourself. Quit thinking about yourself. Love is not proud. It doesn't focus on self. It focuses on God and others.

Question for dialogue: What are some of the ways we focus on ourselves too much, instead of focusing on God or each

142

other? Does my pridefulness show up in thinking too highly of myself, or in thinking too lowly of myself?

Prayer for both of us: Lord, help us no to think of ourselves too much, either too highly, or too lowly. Help us to be focused on You first, then each other. Forgive our pridefulness. Replace it with humility, focusing on the well-being of others first.

Journal...

LOVE IS NOT RUDE

"Love is patient, love is kind. It does not envy, it does not boast, it is not proud. It is not rude, it is not self-seeking, it is not easily angered, it keeps no record of wrongs. Love does not delight in evil but it rejoices with the truth. It always protects, always trusts, always hopes, always perseveres. Love never fails. . . . "—1 Corinthians 13:4-8

The word "rude" suggests something rough, unpolished or unfinished. Love is not rude because it is not rough, unpolished, or unfinished. Love is perfect because God is love, and God is perfect. We, human beings, are often rough, unpolished, and unfinished. To the extent that we demonstrate rudeness we demonstrate just how rough, or immature, we really are. Rudeness is exactly that: immaturity, or an undeveloped character. As a person grows, and matures, as they become fashioned over time by the hand of their Creator, they learn how to use self-control to be a blessing to others. They learn how to prefer others over themselves. They learn how to be more concerned with the other person's feelings than their own. Rudeness grows out of self-centered undeveloped character. I don't care how long you've called yourself a Christian, the bottom line is, if you're still rude to each other, to your children, or to anyone else, you are still self-centered, rough, unpolished and undeveloped as a person created in God's image. Love is not rude because love is complete, finished, polished! True love can only really be shared by grown-ups.

Question for dialogue: How grown-up are we when we measure ourselves by how rude we are to one another? When do we tend to fall into rudeness?

Prayer for both of us: Lord, help us to grow up, spiritually, and emotionally, just as we have intellectually and physically.

Help us to be not rough, but finished and polished by Your own hand.

Journal . . .

LOVE IS NOT SELF-SEEKING

"Love is patient, love is kind. It does not envy, it does not boast, it is not proud. It is not rude, <u>it is not self-seeking,</u> it is not easily angered, it keeps no record of wrongs. Love does not delight in evil but it rejoices with the truth. It always protects, always trusts, always hopes, always perseveres. Love never fails. . . ."—1 Corinthians 13:4-8

It seems like ever since the 1960's, Americans have been on some quest to find themselves. Over thirty years later the fruit of our labors is evident: People are more lost, more confused, more clueless than ever. This new philosophy obviously is a loser. Secular therapists who haven't found themselves yet, are simply helping more people get more lost every day. Jesus gave us the answer two thousand years ago (but of course, we're too sophisticated to believe a carpenter's son who has no letters after his name). Basically He said, "If you really want to find yourself, lose yourself, then you'll find yourself" (my paraphrase). Give yourself to serving others, and your own needs and desires will be met. Give yourself to serving your spouse's needs. Be a blessing, not a source of tension. Forget about yourself, your wants, your needs or even your rights. The only thing we have a right to is to spend an eternity in hell for our sin, where the fire is not quenched and the worm does not die! Thank God, He doesn't treat us according to our rights. If He were really fair we would each hang for our own sin. That's fair! But instead, Jesus saw our need. He didn't seek His own will. He was fully human, and as such, really didn't want to go through what He did, but He concluded, ". . . nevertheless, not my will be done but thine," and He went to the cross. Then God raised Him from the dead and gave Him total victory. That's the way it works. Forget about yourself. Give yourself up for others, and then God will give you the victory that you've been fighting so hard to get on your own. You can keep demanding your rights, fighting for what you think you deserve, but that just isn't love. Love is being a God-seeker, not a self-seeker. Live to serve your spouse and family, and you will have it all—promise!

Question for dialogue: How do we get into demanding our own rights, and get into a contest for who is going to get their own way? What rights do we really think we have?

Prayer for both of us: Lord, help us realize the truth—that every breath we take is a gift of Your grace. Help us to choose every day, and in every word we speak, to seek Your will, not our own. Help us to be God-seekers, not self-seekers.

Journal . . .

LOVE IS NOT EASILY ANGERED

"Love is patient, love is kind. It does not envy, it does not boast, it is not proud. It is not rude, it is not self-seeking, <u>it is not easily angered,</u> it keeps no record of wrongs. Love does not delight in evil but it rejoices with the truth. It always protects, always trusts, always hopes, always perseveres. Love never fails. . . ."—1 Corinthians 13:4-8

Anger is not, in itself, a bad thing. Jesus was angry at the temple when He turned the tables of the moneychangers, yet we know He was without sin. Scripture tell us: "Be angry and sin not." So anger isn't the problem. It's the object and expression of the anger that gets us into trouble. If we find that we are easily angered the problem may be that we aren't just a person who gets angry, but we are an "angry person." There's a big difference. An angry person is one who is filled with anger because of some perceived injustice, which they believe in their hearts, was perpetrated on them. Very often it has to do with a sense of loss, perhaps the loss of a significant person, or a missed opportunity. In either case, they become like a volcano waiting to erupt at the slightest agitation, because in their hearts they believe they got a raw deal. These people become unapproachable and incapable of having a healthy loving relationship. Love is not easily angered. If you are easily angered you cannot love. If you are an angry person you do not have the ability to love. It's impossible to love. If you want to love you need to resolve the anger. Identify it. Bring it into the light where the blood of Jesus is available to bring forgiveness, cleansing and new hope (1 John 1:7, 8). Only then can you begin to receive God's love for yourself and have it to give to others. Until then, you remain an angry, emotionally handicapped person. If you can honestly say you aren't an angry person, but you do get easily angered, then

148

check your expectations. Either others aren't giving what you expect, or they are giving what you don't expect. In either case, your expectations need to be readjusted.

Question for dialogue: Are we easily angered? Are we approachable? Are we people who get angry, or are we angry people? Where do we need to adjust our expectations?

Prayer for both of us: Lord, help us to resolve our anger issues so that we may be capable of having a loving relationship. Bring into the light any hidden source of anger so that we may deal with it and move forward.

Journal . . .

LOVE KEEPS NO RECORD OF WRONGS

"Love is patient, love is kind. It does not envy, it does not boast, it is not proud. It is not rude, it is not self-seeking, it is not easily angered, <u>it keeps no record of wrongs.</u> Love does not delight in evil but it rejoices with the truth. It always protects, always trusts, always hopes, always perseveres. Love never fails. . . ."—1 Corinthians 13:4-8

Did you ever wonder if your spouse had a recorded list, somewhere, of all the things you ever did wrong in all your years of marriage? Does it seem like whenever you have an argument, or you do something wrong, out comes that list of offenses—half of which you already forgot? How will you ever live down the past? There's nothing you can do about it. You can change now, but if you mess up, out comes that list of past offenses. How could he or she remember them the way they do? It seems like they really have them recorded somewhere just waiting for you to mess up, doesn't it? Well, guess what—they do! These offenses are all recorded in the brain. If you could open up your spouse's head and look inside—yours too for that matter—you'll find a file cabinet in there with a bunch of folders, listed with each offense you committed since you first met. It is a record of wrongs. Whenever you mess up out comes the appropriate folder with a whole set of similar offenses to prove you're a serial offender. "You'll never change!" As long as that file cabinet exists you're sunk. Forget it. Guilty!

The only way we can really change is to burn up those files and throw out the file cabinet in our minds. Then there will be no record of wrongs to keep bringing us back when we want to move forward as a new creation. But are we really willing to burn the files and throw out the file cabinet? You may as well ask, "Am I really willing to love?" After all, that's what love is—burning the files and throwing out the file cabinet in your mind. Hold no record of wrongs. Otherwise you're doomed to live in the failures of the past. Yes, it can be scary. It takes faith. But guess what? God has done exactly that for us. He holds no file cabinet with our sins neatly filed away. Isn't that a relief! That's the least we can do for each other. As God loves us, let us love one another; Let us throw out the old file cabinet once and for all, so that no matter what our past was, our future will be a blank page. Love holds no record of wrongs.

Question for dialogue: Does it really seem like we have a file cabinet in our minds that provides us ammunition to accuse one another of our hurtful past?

Prayer for both of us: Lord, help us to burn up the old files and throw out the file cabinet in our minds. Help us to hold no record of wrongs against one another. Help us to start new every morning to walk in newness of life.

Journal . . .

LOVE DOES NOT DELIGHT IN EVIL

"Love is patient, love is kind. It does not envy, it does not boast, it is not proud. It is not rude, it is not self-seeking, it is not easily angered, it keeps no record of wrongs. <u>*Love does not delight in evil*</u> *but it rejoices with the truth. It always protects, always trusts, always hopes, always perseveres. Love never fails. . . ."*—1 Corinthians 13:4-8

We don't usually think of ourselves as people who would delight in evil, but when was the last time you've gloated over someone else's misfortune? When was the last time you thought, "I'm glad it's not me"? Did you delight in the fact that it was someone else? When your husband or wife made a mistake and had to suffer the consequences of that mistake, were you supportive, or did the look on your face tell your spouse "I told you so!"? Love doesn't delight in evil; neither does it make excuses or allowances. Love mourns over evil. It is saddened by sin. Love doesn't gloat. It hurts with the hurts of others.

Imagine a person falling into a ditch. Finding himself at the bottom he looks up, and there sees a friend looking down on him. Then the friend says, "How did you fall into that ditch? Were you drunk or something? Just climb out. It can't be that hard. I told you don't be hanging around open ditches anyway!" Then you see Jesus. Jesus doesn't say a word. He just climbs down into the ditch, comes alongside the person and helps him up until he's safely out. Jesus is our model. Let's not gloat over our spouse's misfortunes, or rejoice that it's not us, or be quick to pass judgment. Let's simply get down into the ditch and gently help each other to recover and find healing. Let's be Jesus to one another.

Question for dialogue: Do I feel supported by you when I fall, or do I feel like you gloat, or are quick to judge me? Do I feel that you delight when I make a mistake?

Prayer for both of us: Lord, help us to be sensitive to one another's hurts. Help us to remember that we need to make it together. Help us not to delight in seeing each other fall, but help us to be a lifter upper, not a put downer.

Journal . . .

LOVE REJOICES WITH TRUTH

"Love is patient, love is kind. It does not envy, it does not boast, it is not proud. It is not rude, it is not self-seeking, it is not easily angered, it keeps no record of wrongs. Love does not delight in evil but it rejoices with the truth. It always protects, always trusts, always hopes, always perseveres. Love never fails. . . ."—1 Corinthians 13:4-8

Isn't it interesting how Paul doesn't contrast evil with good in this passage, but instead he contrasts it with truth. On the one hand you have evil, and on the other, you have not good, but truth! That's because truth is good! "But the truth of my situation isn't so good," you might say. "In fact, the truth of my situation is pretty lousy!" I hear you. But let's first understand that no matter what your situation looks like, you're only seeing part of it. The truth of it goes beyond what you see. Truth has a name. It's Jesus! He said, "I am the Way, the Truth, and the Life" (John 14:6). Jesus is the Truth of your situation. And to the extent that your situation is in Jesus, to that extent it's good, regardless of what you see! Please don't be one of those weird, normal people (talk about an oxymoron!) who are limited by physical reality. The truth goes beyond what you see. That's why it's good! The truth is that no matter what you see Jesus really is able to bring it to a good report. He really is able to do the impossible. He really is able to take our mess, and do something beautiful with it—if we'll only let Him. That's why no matter where we're at we can rejoice with the Truth—with Jesus! Love stays focused, not on our situation but on Jesus. He is the One who is able to do what we can't, who can provide what we need, who can lift us up when we're down, who can give us the love we need for each other—a love we just don't have in the natural.

154

So whatever is yet in the darkness, whether it be thoughts, feelings or actions, let's bring it all into the light of God's love—the light of truth, where the blood of Jesus flows to forgive and fellowship can be restored.

The truth is that _**we can do all things through Christ who strengthens us**_. Rejoice!!

Questions for dialogue:What is the truth of our marriage? What is it that we need Jesus to do for us that we just don't have the power to do within ourselves? What is the true testimony that we will pass on to our children that will demonstrate the validity of our faith, and the goodness of God?

Prayer for both of us: Lord, help us to not focus on the problems in our marriage, but on the truth. Help us to rejoice with Jesus. Help us to stay focused on truth as we bring things into the light by the power and comfort of your Holy Spirit.

Journal . . .

LOVE ALWAYS PROTECTS

"Love is patient, love is kind. It does not envy, it does not boast, it is not proud. It is not rude, it is not self-seeking, it is not easily angered, it keeps no record of wrongs. Love does not delight in evil but it rejoices with the truth. It always protects, always trusts, always hopes, always perseveres. Love never fails. . . . "—1 Corinthians 13:4-8

If love always protects, and I say I love my spouse, then it ought to be true that I always protect her. I protect her when she's in physical danger. That's basic. But I also should be protecting her from emotional injury as well. When others say something derogatory about my wife do I just "let it slide" or do I protect her so that others will know that they dare not say one negative word about my wife in my presence? Do I really protect my spouse from hurtful words of others? Do I protect my spouse from my own hurtful words? Am I approachable? Is it emotionally safe to talk about anything with me, or is it a matter of walking on eggshells? Let's be honest. Could it be that I am the greatest source of emotional hurt in my spouse's life? If that's the case, then perhaps I don't have a clue about what real love is—a love that always, *always* protects. If I'm not protecting her from my own hurtful words as much as I possibly can, then I'm really not loving my wife, regardless of what I would like to think. That's the gospel truth—the bottom line.

Do I protect my spouse from being overworked by the job, or by the children to the point where they are so stressed they are always on edge? Am I willing to protect my spouse in every way? Am I willing to do whatever it takes to insure their physical, emotional, and most importantly, their spiritual safety? "It's too much," you say. "I can't do all that. It's

156

impossible." You're right. The only way to protect your spouse to this degree is to draw upon a resource greater than yourself. It will have to come from God. If you don't have the resources to always protect, then you don't have the resources to love. Go get them. Go to the well. Receive God's supernatural love and protection for yourself. Only then will you have it to give to your spouse. A love that always protects is not natural. It's supernatural. It can only come from a supernatural God. That's love.

Questions for dialogue: What ways do we feel protected by one another? What ways do we feel unprotected? Do we feel unprotected against each other? Against others? Against our circumstances? How can we help one another feel more protected physically, emotionally and spiritually?

Prayer for both of us: Lord, help us to protect one another against hurtful words of others, unhealthy situations, and above all, help us protect each other from ourselves. Help us to always—*always*—protect.

Journal . . .

LOVE ALWAYS TRUSTS

"Love is patient, love is kind. It does not envy, it does not boast, it is not proud. It is not rude, it is not self-seeking, it is not easily angered, it keeps no record of wrongs. Love does not delight in evil but it rejoices with the truth. It always protects, <u>always trusts</u>, always hopes, always perseveres. Love never fails. . . ."—1 Corinthians 13:4-8

Love always trusts. Boy, that's a tough one! How can I trust my spouse after I've been hurt so much? Why should I trust when I see no reason to think he or she will ever change, or even wants to change? Won't I just be setting myself up for further disappointment if I trust my spouse, and I'm hurt again?

Those are some pretty valid questions, and the truth of the matter is that most of us aren't really trustworthy anyway. To put your trust in a spouse who isn't trustworthy makes no sense. You will be hurt again, and become more bitter and angry. Your condition will be worse in the end than it was in the beginning. God isn't calling you to put your trust in a person who is either unable, or unwilling to honor that trust. That's simply misplaced trust. That's not love. Then what does the word mean when it says love always trusts? It simply means that when I can't trust my spouse I can *trust God for my spouse.* Even if my spouse is being unfaithful I can trust that God is working on their hearts and minds to bring them to their senses as I pray for God's will to be done which is always restoration. It means that in the areas I can't trust my spouse I can trust God for my spouse. I can, therefore, always trust. It may mean pressing into God as never before. You can't trust someone you don't know to be trustworthy. You must press into God until you know how trustworthy He

158

really is. You can only do this through worship, prayer and reading the Word. Develop an intimate and personal relationship with God so that you can trust Him to keep your spouse, and to be working in your spouse's heart and mind. Know Him so that you can trust He is working in both of you to give you a marriage He can display to the world as His handiwork. Love always trusts. You can love, because you can always trust, if not in your spouse, then in the God who is watching over your spouse.

Question for dialogue: What areas do I feel I can trust you for? What areas do I feel I can only trust God for?

Prayer for both of us: Lord help us to develop a trust in You that is greater than all our fears and anxieties, knowing that as we grow in trust in You for our marriage we will also grow in a healthy trust in one another.

Journal . . .

LOVE ALWAYS HOPES

"Love is patient, love is kind. It does not envy, it does not boast, it is not proud. It is not rude, it is not self-seeking, it is not easily angered, it keeps no record of wrongs. Love does not delight in evil but it rejoices with the truth. It always protects, always trusts, <u>always hopes</u>, always perseveres. Love never fails. . . ."—1 Corinthians 13:4-8

The writer of Hebrews tells us that we have this hope (the hope of His promises) as an anchor for the soul, firm and secure (Heb 6:19a). We all need to be anchored in a firm and secure truth that will keep us steady in uncertain times and stormy seasons in our relationships. Otherwise we may find ourselves adrift in a sea of confusion, discouragement and aimlessness. If we let go of the dream we had when we said, "I do" there's no knowing where we will end up. More often than not, we'll find ourselves tossed on the sands of a foreign land, lost and afraid.

But love always hopes. It's always anchored in the promises of God—the promises we believed when we said "I do." That's our anchor. That's what will keep us steady and focused, not on the stormy seas, but on the clearing beyond the horizon. God's promises are still good. That's why we can hope, and why that hope will not disappoint us if we will persevere. No matter how long the night, the sun will still rise, and God's promises are still good. That is the anchor for my soul.

<u>*Questions for both of us:*</u> What were the hopes and dreams we had when we were first married? What will our marriage and family look like when these hopes become reality?

160

Prayer for both of us: Lord, help us to continue to stay anchored and unmoved in our faith to see Your promises become reality. Help us to continue to place our hopes and dreams in Your goodness, and keep our focus on the realization of that hope.

Journal . . .

LOVE ALWAYS PERSEVERES

"Love is patient, love is kind. It does not envy, it does not boast, it is not proud. It is not rude, it is not self-seeking, it is not easily angered, it keeps no record of wrongs. Love does not delight in evil but it rejoices with the truth. It always protects, always trusts, always hopes, <u>always perseveres</u>. Love never fails. . . ."—1 Corinthians 13:4-8

The world's ways are abort, divorce and cop out. God's ways are ***commit, submit and don't quit***. I was recently blessed by an e-mail from a former client who found us on the web and wanted to let us know that she had taken that counsel to heart, and as a result succeeded in making it to the top 2% of her company's sales force. Besides her success in business, their marriage has been restored and they are building a brand new home.

This formula is the key to success whether we're talking about business or relationships, whether we're talking about our careers or our marriages. I can't tell you how often I felt like quitting when things got rough between Penny and myself. It seemed like things would never change. Whenever we started talking about real issues it seemed to just get worse. Why bother? But we had closed the back door in our minds. There was no way out. Divorce wasn't an option. First we had to commit to the goal of restoration, and a love based in honesty and openness. We had to commit to achieving the marriage we both knew God wanted us to have. Then we had to submit to doing whatever it would take to see that happen. That was tough for me. I'm not very good at submitting to anything, or anybody. I guess I had a problem with that pride thing—typical guy! Ultimately, I had to accept the fact that God did know more than me. His ways were better than mine.

How do you like that? Then it was a matter of persevering; working through the issues, trying to communicate, getting angry, asking forgiveness, then doing it all over again, and again and again. It was tough, but we didn't give up. We didn't cop out. We didn't divorce. By our choice and God's power we persevered, and God brought us through. Hallelujah! That's one trip I never want to go on again. But what we have now is worth all the work, strain and pain we went through. We have love—real honest to goodness love for each other, freely and willingly given. It's great! But we never would have seen it had we quit. Thank God we didn't. Our kids are pretty grateful too. Persevere. Commit, submit and don't quit. It works!

Question for dialogue: When do I feel like I want to quit? When do I feel you want to quit?

Prayer for both of us: Lord, give us the power to persevere; to commit to the marriage, to submit to do whatever it takes, then to stick to it until we see the fulfillment of Your promise to bring restoration, righteousness, peace and joy.

Journal . . .

LOVE NEVER FAILS

:Love is patient, love is kind. It does not envy, it does not boast, it is not proud. It is not rude, it is not self-seeking, it is not easily angered, it keeps no record of wrongs. Love does not delight in evil but it rejoices with the truth. It always protects, always trusts, always hopes, always perseveres. <u>Love never fails. . . .</u>"—1 Corinthians 13:4-8

Today, Penny and I can look back over more than thirty years of marriage, and all the trials we've been through. It's been a long tough road, but has it been worth it? Let me share with you the pre-printed portion of a card Penny just sent me. (She sends me cards even though we work together in the same office. The personal stuff she wrote I'll keep personal):

"I wish we could run away,
find some little uninhabited island,
And just make love to each other day and night
for the rest of our lives. . . .
I know that's selfish,
but sometimes the pressures and responsibilities
of daily life leave us so little time and energy for spending
time together,
And in my mind, that's the most important thing of all.
I love you so very much!
So please don't ever think for a moment
that you're not my first priority,
because no matter where I am,
or what I'm doing, in my heart,
I'm on that little island with you,
loving you until the end of time."

When I eventually got my composure back after reading that (Who said big men don't cry?) I realized the truth of God's word, "Love never . . . never . . . never . . . fails!" For all that we've been through, for all that we've never acquired or accomplished, we have seen the fulfillment of God's promise: We have love. All the money in the world, all the worldly success, nothing could buy what Jesus bought for us on the cross—the ability to love with his unconditional, limitless love, a love that truly never fails! Whatever we've been through, it's been worth it, because, by His grace, we have love—real love.

Question for dialogue: How have we seen God's love come through for us over the years?

Prayer for both of us: "Lord, help us to continue to walk in Your unconditional love for one another. Help us keep each other at the very top of our priority list right under Your name. Help us to demonstrate that love to our children and those in our sphere of influence. Thank You so much for giving us the greatest Gift ever given—Your love, whose name is Jesus."

Journal . . .

Storms

PREPARING FOR THE STORM

"The LORD will not leave the guilty unpunished. His way is in the whirlwind and the storm, and clouds are the dust of his feet." "When the storm has swept by, the wicked are gone, but the righteous stand firm forever."—Nahum 1:3; Proverbs 10:25

Here we are in the first week of March, and the weather forecast is calling for the biggest snowstorm in decades. Talk about March coming in like a lion! Well, I guess we have to accept the fact that we can't control the weather. But we can control how we make it through by being sure we're prepared. You know, stock up on groceries, flashlight batteries, bottled water, etc.

Relationships are much the same. Storms come up at the most inconvenient times. Unfortunately, we haven't yet invented Doppler radar to foresee storms in relationships. But if you stop to think about it, there may be ways you can observe the atmospheric conditions in the relationship, and predict, with some degree of accuracy, a coming storm. Then again, maybe the storm comes out of nowhere, totally unforeseen or unexpected. Whether we can see it coming or not, the key to making it through the storm is all about preparation. Are we sufficiently joined together in prayer? Are we sufficiently open and honest with one another about our thoughts and feelings so that no whirlwind in our minds will conjure up vane or hurtful imaginations? Have we made sufficient deposits into one another's love bank that our account balance is sufficiently high to endure the toughest of storms? Are we clothed in the righteousness of Christ, together, where we can find shelter from the storm?

If we're not anchored in Him the gale force winds can easily blow us away. As long as there is weather there will be storms. Be prepared. Keep love bank account balances up, stay anchored in Christ, and you will be prepared for the storm—no matter when it comes.

Question for both of us: What are the atmospheric conditions in our home? What are some of the things that give away the fact that a storm may be coming? How can we be better prepared? Are our love bank balances sufficiently high to endure a storm? Are we anchored in Christ together?

Prayer for both of us: Lord, help us to be prepared for the next storm. Help us to be anchored in You together. Help us to work at making deposits into one another's love bank so that our account balances will be sufficiently high to endure the next storm. Help us to stand in Your righteousness, firm forever.

Journal . . .

THROUGH THE STORM

"Without warning, a furious storm came up on the lake, so that the waves swept over the boat. But Jesus was sleeping. The disciples went and woke him, saying, 'Lord, save us! We're going to drown!' He replied, 'You of little faith, why are you so afraid?' Then he got up and rebuked the winds and the waves, and it was completely calm. The men were amazed and asked, 'What kind of man is this? Even the winds and the waves obey him!' "—Matthew 8:24-27

The "storm of the decade" the weather prognosticators warned us about last week never happened. Thank God! We've had enough of winter this year. Nevertheless there were many storms this weekend, not outside, but inside the homes of couples and families struggling to find a sense of peace and order for their lives. Instead, they often find themselves like the waves of a storm driven sea, tossed every which way. There seems to be no rest.

The disciples were actually with Jesus when a storm came their way, and they reacted as many of us would—in fear. Sometimes, in our personal relationships, we express our fear in anger, or depression. Actually, depression is anger. It's anger turned inward. If we react in anger we simply feed the storm and it grows in intensity until it blows us away. During a 48-hour weekend, according to latest statistics, 6,000 families in our nation have succumbed to the storm drowning in the sea of divorce. What's the answer? How do we make it through the storms of strife, anger, frustration and fear?

Hebrews 6:19 tells us: *"We have this hope as an anchor for the soul, firm and secure."* The key is to be anchored securely in Christ. The storm may come, but we can ride it out, as we take a deep breath of the Holy Spirit, and allow ourselves to simply ride out the ocean swells in our souls until we feel our feet touching firm ground once again. Don't panic. Don't flail around. Don't fight those trying to make it through the storm with you; especially those who may be trying to rescue you! Simply be anchored in your hope in Christ. Regardless of what may be in the wind and the waves, ride it out in grace and truth. It will pass, and you will be on firm ground again, if you are anchored in Him. He is the shelter. And believe it or not, something good comes out of the storm.

Question for both of us: How frequent, or infrequent, are the storms inside our home? How do we tend to react, in fear? Anger? Frustration? Who seems to get hurt the most when these storms come? Why?

Prayer for both of us: Lord, help us to learn to be anchored in the hope of Jesus when the next storm comes through our relationship. Help us stay steady, anchored in Christ, and in the knowledge that regardless of what we see with our eyes, He is still in control of the seas and the wind. With Jesus in our boat we will make it through the storm.

Journal . . .

AFTER THE STORM

"When the storm has swept by, the wicked are gone, but the righteous stand firm forever."—Proverbs 10:25

Every adversity has the seed of a greater benefit. When the storms come in our own lives—and they will—and after we have done all we can to be prepared, and after, by His grace and power, we make it through to the other side, what are we left with? Are we left with a greater sense of division, brokenness, disappointment and anger because of the storm, or do we sense more oneness with our spouse, a deeper intimacy, a greater love, because we went through the storm together? We have been through some pretty tough storms in our marriage, but the one thing we have purposed in our hearts to do is to go through the storms together. No longer do we want to isolate ourselves from one another, because we're too proud to admit we need each other. No longer do we insist on making it through "on our own." We need Jesus. We need each other. After the storm, when the winds have died down, and the waves have settled, we can look back together and see what of our carnal nature God has washed away in the storm. We can allow Jesus to bring healing to both of us together. Then we can celebrate the very fact that we made it through, and we're just a little more like Jesus after the storm then we were before.

When you see the storm clouds gathering, do all you can to be prepared, and then hang on to each other, in His righteousness. Know that God will speak to you in the storm, but you need to listen carefully. Know that God is allowing the adversity to bring forth the seed of a greater benefit—to draw you closer to Him and to one another.

Question for both of us: Think of the last storm we've been through in our relationship. What was it of our carnal nature that God was trying to wash away in the storm? How did we feel when it was all over? Did we feel closer for having gone through it together?

Prayer for both of us: Lord, help us to look back on the storms in our lives and relationships with a redemptive eye. Help us to come through together, growing closer and experiencing Your healing together. Help us to remain standing firm in Your righteousness just a bit more conformed to Your image, because of the storm we've been through together.

Journal . . .

PRAYER FOR OUR MARRIAGE

Father, marriage is Your idea. It is one of Your divinely created institutions based on the idea of covenant. We have entered into that covenant freely, and do hereby commit ourselves to do whatever it takes to be good stewards of this covenant that You might receive the glory. We confess our sinfulness and self-centered ways and choose to do Your will. It is written in Your Word that love is shed abroad in our hearts by the Holy Ghost who is given to us. Because You are in us, we acknowledge that love reigns supreme. We believe that love is displayed in full expression enfolding and knitting us together in truth, making us perfect for every good work to do Your will and working in us that which is pleasing in Your sight.

We live and conduct ourselves, and our marriage honorably and becomingly. We esteem it as precious, worthy and of great value. We commit ourselves to live in harmony and in one accord. We delight in each other, being of the same mind and united in spirit.

Father, we believe and say that we are gentle, compassionate, courteous, tender-hearted and humble-minded. We seek peace and it keeps our hearts in quietness and assurance. We are heirs together of the grace of God.

Our marriage grows stronger day by day in the bond of unity because it is founded on Your Word and rooted and grounded in Your love. Father, we thank You for the performance of it, in Jesus' name.

REFERENCES:
Romans 5:5   Philippians 1:9   Colosssians 3:14   Colossians 1:10
Philippians 2:13   Philippians 2:2   Ephesians 4:32   Isaiah 32:17
Philippians 4:7   I Peter 3:7   Ephesians 3:17-18   Jeremiah 1:12

TO BE A CHRISTIAN

To be a Christian is not a matter of formal religion, but a matter of personal relationship with Jesus Christ. One of the reasons marriage was given to us was to provide an example of what our relationship should be with Christ.

When we said, "I do" it was supposed to represent a life-long commitment to another person, to give that person number one place in our hearts. Well, to be a Christian means to say, "I do" to Jesus Christ, and give Him that number one place. A Christian is, quite simply, a person who has placed Jesus Christ in that very special place in their hearts—number one. You can know if you are a Christian and have the promise of eternal life by simply looking into your heart and asking, "Who is number one?" If it's yourself, another person, your job, or even a formal religion, you do not have the promise of salvation. It's time to dethrone that idol and place Jesus Christ in His rightful place. You can say a simple prayer like this; be sure it comes from your heart.

Dear Heavenly Father,

I confess that You have not been number one in my life. I'm sorry. Please forgive me. Jesus Christ, come into my life; cleanse me of my sin and take Your rightful place on the throne of my life. No longer will I ask You to bless my life so that I can live it the way I want. From this day forward I seek Your plan for my life and will try to live it according to Your Word. Give me the wisdom to know Your will, and the power, by Your Spirit, to live for You.

Thank You, Jesus, for hearing my prayer. Thank You for dying on the cross to pay the penalty for my sin. Thank You for new and everlasting life.—Amen.

If you have prayed this prayer please drop us an e-mail and let us know. It's most important that you plant yourself in a Bible-believing church and begin to grow. This is only the beginning of an exciting and wonderful journey into the fullness of His love. In fact, you can't really know love until you know God.

To order more of these Couples' Devotionals, or to find out about setting up a Marriage Saver Seminar for your church contact us:

Marriage and Family Savers Ministries
229 Robinson Ave.
Newburgh, NY 12550

Web site

www.marriageandfamily.org,

or call toll-free

1-877-MSAVERS